"A valuable addition to your ACT toolkit."

—**Russ Harris**, author of *The Happiness Trap*

"ACT has burst upon the psychotherapy scene with creativity, a deep sense of excitement, and, most importantly, strong empirical support. With its premise that human suffering is an unfortunate byproduct of our everyday language and conceptions, metaphors become a more important tool in this therapeutic approach than most others. Now, Jill A. Stoddard, and Niloofar Afari have assembled these metaphors in an entertaining reference book that will be extraordinarily valuable—not only to practitioners of ACT, but to psychotherapists everywhere."

—**David H. Barlow PhD, ABPP**, professor of psychology and psychiatry at Boston University and founder and director emeritus of the Center for Anxiety and Related Disorders

"As the interest in ACT has grown internationally, there has been a burgeoning desire to find new and individually relevant metaphors and exercises to use across a variety of settings and clinical populations. This book will certainly satisfy that appetite for those looking for new ways to best connect with their clients. But more importantly, this book will inspire readers to recognize what has been true all along: that the metaphors and exercises that will be most useful are those that draw upon clients' own experiences. By bringing this compendium together, the authors will inspire clinicians around the world to be more creative in their practice."

—**Sonja V. Batten, PhD**, president (2013-2014) of the Association for Contextual Behavioral Science and adjunct associate professor of psychiatry at Uniformed Services University of the Health Sciences

"While numerous ACT textbooks and workbooks are available, this book is essential for any current or future ACT practitioner. In addition to including over 100 metaphors and exercises, Stoddard and Afari have beautifully organized the content in this book and matched each exercise or metaphor with its respective core process (e.g., values, committed action). The authors go above and beyond to cite the source from which the material was collected and even provide specific page numbers in order to assist the reader in obtaining previously published material. The inclusion of material that can be used for both group counseling and individual sessions represents a strength of the book. Each chapter is concise, easy to read, and detailed enough for even the most novice counselor to replicate in session."

—**The Professional Counselor**, December 2014

THE
BIG BOOK
of ACT
METAPHORS

A Practitioner's Guide to Experiential Exercises &
Metaphors in Acceptance & Commitment Therapy

JILL A. STODDARD, PHD
NILOOFAR AFARI, PHD

NEW HARBINGER PUBLICATIONS, INC.

Publisher's Note

NEW HARBINGER PUBLICATIONS is a registered trademark of New Harbinger Publications, Inc.

Distributed in Canada by Raincoast Books

Cover design by Amy Shoup
Acquired by Catharine Meyers
Edited by Jasmine Star
Text design by Tracy Marie Carlson
Indexed by James Minkin

Library of Congress Cataloging-in-Publication Data

Stoddard, Jill A.
  The big book of ACT metaphors : a practitioner's guide to experiential exercises and metaphors in acceptance and commitment therapy / Jill A. Stoddard, PhD, and Niloofar Afari, PhD ; foreword by Steven C. Hayes.
      pages cm
  Summary: "The use of metaphors is fundamental in the successful delivery of acceptance and commitment therapy (ACT), but for many ACT therapists, they often become over-used, stale, and less effective as time wears on. The Big Book of ACT Metaphors is an essential A-Z resource guide that includes new metaphors and experiential exercises to help promote client acceptance, defusion from troubling thoughts, and values-based action. The book also includes scripts tailored to different client populations. Whether treating a client with anxiety, depression, trauma, or an eating disorder, this book will provide mental health professionals with the skills needed to improve lives, one exercise at a time"-- Provided by publisher.
  Includes bibliographical references and index.
  ISBN 978-1-60882-529-5 (paperback) -- ISBN 978-1-60882-530-1 (pdf e-book) -- ISBN 978-1-60882-531-8 (epub) 1. Acceptance and commitment therapy. I. Afari, Niloofar. II. Title.
  RC489.A32S63 2014
  616.89'14--dc23
                                    2014000026

Printed in the United States of America

23   22   21

20   19   18   17   16   15   14

To Billy, Scarlett, and Chips: all my sweet spots start and end with you.

—JS

To my loving family: Seth, Matine, and Kian, you are my inspirations for a life of acceptance and commitment.

—NA

We must accept life for what it actually is—a challenge to our quality without which we should never know of what stuff we are made, or grow to our full stature.

—Ida Wylie

CONTENTS

FOREWORD

Metaphors and Human Liberation

The vast majority of human language is metaphorical. Language did not evolve in order for humans to explore their psyche, or understand their deep feelings. Indeed, there was a time when it was difficult or perhaps impossible even to speak of a psyche. Or understanding. Or feelings.

"Psyche" is a metaphor, frozen in place long ago. It comes from a word for breathing—and psyche was what was presumed to energize the breath. "Breath energy" was as close as speakers could come to the idea.

"Understanding" was literally "standing under"—making a report as a messenger would, standing below the king in his high throne and, as we say, "laying it out."

There was once no word even for something as basic as "feeling." The word was a metaphorical extension from the word for "hand." You have to imagine a time when to talk of feeling a feeling you had to say the equivalent of "you know, what the hand does."

Language evolved originally to deal with issues of blood and bone—not abstract concepts. The simple bidirectional relationship between objects and their names allowed an extension of speaker and listener roles, enormously increasing our capacity for cooperation. As this tribal species called human beings learned to use symbols, the capacity for reason, problem solving, and imagination grew. We added new cognitive relations. Cultural development began with a vengeance.

The accelerator in that process was metaphor. Through metaphor, we could take an existing network of knowledge, the vehicle, and bring it to bear on a new domain, the target. If the vehicle contained relations and functions that were missing in the target, and if the link between the two was apt, entire networks of knowledge could be transferred to new areas in the length of time it took to tell a story or draw an analogy.

With that new process in hand, we had the cognitive tool we needed to transform human life. We could construct subtle differences, or extend similar forms.

The importance of this process to human knowledge and human development is revealed in the ubiquity of frozen metaphors, such as those I have just described. But it is also revealed in how extensively we use stories and metaphors within education and in psychotherapy.

Good psychotherapists are good storytellers. They know how to open clients up to what is truly new by using knowledge that is old. They know how to create experiences that inform and heal.

What you have in your hands is the result of the creative work of hundreds of clinicians doing just that. Even if they are not in this volume in a named way, this volume stands atop their work. ACT therapists deal daily with subtle and yet important psychological postures that lie at the interface between direct experience and human language.

ACT is attempting to change the relationship between people and their own psychological content. ACT seeks to rein in the excesses of such language processes as judgment, prediction, problem solving, comparison, self-evaluation, and planning. People can become lost in their own verbal processes and, because of that, fail to see or to respond to their own experience or to the context in which they live. ACT helps us see an alternative.

Changing that relationship cannot be done in the same frame of mind that produced the unhealthy relationship to begin with. You cannot judge judgment and thereby rein it in. You cannot solve the problem of excess problem solving with more mental analysis and verbal problem solving.

Metaphors and exercises are verbal, but they are not literal, evaluative, or analytical. Their messages are inherently softer, more subtle, and more individualistic than logical syllogisms or strict rules of performance. Metaphors and exercises are stories and experiences that link the richness of what you already know to domains in which you are unsure what to do.

This remarkable book contains a rich mix of metaphors and exercises that comprise new ways to talk about and to explore important clinical topics in ACT and related forms of therapy. These stories and exercises will stick with you—and they will stick with your clients. When you do not know which way to turn with a client, these simple but clear processes will shine a light forward and give you new territory to explore.

That is exactly what metaphors have done for the human species for thousands of years. Harnessing metaphors and exercises in clinical work is just putting this remarkable capability to its highest use. These are metaphors of human liberation.

—Steven C. Hayes
Foundation Professor and Director of Clinical Training
University of Nevada, Reno
September 2013

ACKNOWLEDGMENTS

First and foremost, we would like to extend an enormous amount of gratitude and appreciation to everyone in the ACT community who expressed excitement about this project and especially those who contributed metaphors and exercises. The best part of writing this book was receiving e-mails from all over the world from fellow ACT-ors who were willing to generously share their creative and unique ideas. This is a very special group, and they make the world better one client, trainee, or research participant at a time.

We also would like to thank our mentors and friends, among them Steve Hayes, Robyn Walser, Kelly Wilson, Jacque Pistorello, Nancy Taylor, Sue Orsillo, Liz Roemer, and the folks at the Center for Anxiety and Related Disorders at Boston University. They are among the most talented and inspiring folks we know, and we are beyond grateful for their influence on us and on the field.

Matthieu Villatte, Jennifer Villatte, and Jean-Louis Monestès deserve special appreciation for their contribution to this book by writing chapter 2. In addition, our students and colleagues were a source of ideas and support throughout; some of them provided materials and are listed as chapter coauthors.

Our deepest thanks also go to John Helmer, Mark Stern, and Christina Zeitountsyan. Without their tireless efforts this book could not possibly have come to fruition. We are forever in their debt for the hours upon hours of tedious but necessary assistance they provided, and we are grateful for their enthusiasm and support.

We also would like to acknowledge the folks at New Harbinger. They provided the helpful guidance a couple of first-time book writers need, and did so not only with patience, but with tremendous enthusiasm.

Finally, our families deserve our deepest gratitude for their patience and understanding while we were locked away writing, their support when we were anxiously sweating our deadlines, and their confidence in us when we were doubting our ability to really do this. Their love and support was truly inspirational. Thank you.

INTRODUCTION

Being human means having feelings of every variety, some we like, and some we don't. Pain, whether physical or emotional, is universal. While pain may feel unpleasant, it is the struggle to escape or avoid pain that most often leads to true suffering. This premise lies at the heart of acceptance and commitment therapy (Hayes, Strosahl, & Wilson, 1999).

What Is Acceptance and Commitment Therapy?

Acceptance and commitment therapy, or ACT (pronounced as the word "act," not the letters a-c-t) is a behavioral therapy that focuses on valued engagement in life. Through six core processes—acceptance and willingness, cognitive defusion, present-moment awareness, self-as-context, values, and committed action—clients are guided to open up and invite all of these experiences in—thoughts and feelings of all varieties, light or dark. ACT advocates opening to internal experiences not because there is some glory in feeling pain for pain's sake, but because efforts to avoid painful feelings—for example by drinking alcohol, being passive in relationships, or avoiding public speaking—create suffering insofar as those efforts pull us away from things that are important to us and that contribute meaning and vitality to our lives. ACT centers on identifying the thoughts and feelings that act as obstacles to valued living and aims to change our relationship to those internal experiences, rather than changing the experiences themselves.

So why use the ACT approach? Because it works and clients like it. Research suggests that ACT is effective with a wide variety of conditions, including eating disorders (Baer, Fischer, & Huss, 2005; Juarascio, Forman, & Herbert, 2010), anxiety disorders (Brown et al., 2011; Vøllestad, Nielsen, & Nielsen, 2011; Roemer, Orsillo, & Salters-Pedneault, 2008), psychosis (Bach & Hayes, 2002), chronic pain (Vowles & McCracken, 2008; Wetherell et al., 2011a), tinnitus (Westin et al., 2011), diabetes management (Gregg, Callaghan, Hayes, & Glenn-Lawson, 2007), skin picking (Twohig, Hayes, & Masuda, 2006), substance use problems (Hayes et al., 2004; Smout et al., 2010), depression (Zettle & Rains, 1989; Bohlmeijer, Fledderus, Rokx, & Pieterse, 2011), and others. Clients also rate ACT with greater satisfaction (Wetherell et al., 2011a) and may drop out less frequently than in some other types of therapies (Wetherell et al., 2011b). In addition, ACT offers a transdiagnostic approach to treatment, allowing it to answer the needs of clients with multiple symptoms, problems, or comorbidities, and making it easier to disseminate to professionals and trainees.

Metaphors and Exercises in ACT

ACT suggests that psychological inflexibility is at the core of human suffering, and that inflexibility arises through entanglement with verbal rules and the traps of language. Through the six core therapeutic processes, clients learn to mitigate the impact of literal language (taking the mind's messages at face value and becoming fused with their content). This creates the wiggle room needed to take actions that are guided by personal values, rather than being driven by internal private events.

If, however, language is at the core of human suffering, how can we use psychotherapy to alleviate suffering, given that the foundation of therapy is verbal dialogue? Of course there is no getting around the need to use oral communication. However, ACT attempts to circumvent some of the problems inherent in literal language by shifting away from traditional didactics and dialogue and moving toward a more experiential encounter. Through mindfulness exercises, clients are encouraged to observe and make contact with their thoughts and emotions as they occur, both in and out of session. In addition, the use of a wide variety of metaphors and experiential exercises is central to helping clients understand the approach in an experienced way, rather than intellectually.

How This Book Came About

That's where this book comes in. We have been practicing, researching, teaching, and supervising ACT for years. Throughout these years, we have had to hunt for metaphors and exercises to use with our clients and trainees by searching through the various resources on our bookshelves, and we have often thought, *Wouldn't it be great to have one book that offers one-stop shopping with scripts for all of the core concepts?* We were especially interested in a resource like this to help our trainees go beyond the classic ACT metaphors and exercises—one that would allow them to create their own scripts tailored to the needs of specific clients. Then, a few years ago, we finally decided to make a bold move and create that resource ourselves.

Perhaps most exciting is the fact that, while we are the authors named on the front cover, this book was really written by the ACT community. We knew that providing the number of novel exercises and metaphors we envisioned would, as they say, require a village. The beauty of the ACT community is that it is comprised of a group of bright, enthusiastic individuals with an impressive record of collaboration and sharing that can be readily observed on the website of the Association for Contextual Behavioral Science (ACBS; http://contextualscience.org), in the many books published by New Harbinger that provide free companion resources, and on the various websites of ACT practitioners. So we reached out to the ACT community via e-mail and the ACBS Listserv asking people to contribute their favorite metaphors and exercises to the book. The response was astounding! We received contributions from all over the world, along with a lot of positive and excited comments about the book. We are immensely grateful to everyone who contributed; without them, this book would not exist. We also thank everyone for allowing us to edit their contributions, sometimes substantially, in the service of creating a more uniform, consistent presentation.

Who This Book Is For

The Big Book of ACT Metaphors is for any professional who practices, researches, teaches, or supervises ACT. Whether you are new to ACT or are a more experienced clinician, this book offers a substantial number of new exercises and metaphors, along with a few classics. This book is not intended for ACT therapy clients; however, scripts may be photocopied and sent home for practice. In the appendices you'll find worksheets to accompany several of the exercises; these are available for you to download at http://www.newharbinger.com/25295. (See the back of this book for more information.)

What You Can Expect in This Book

This is a book designed to supplement existing (and future) ACT protocols by providing clinicians, researchers, and trainees with a one-stop resource for finding (or creating) the perfect metaphor or exercise to demonstrate any of the six core concepts of ACT.

Chapter 1, Overview of ACT, provides a brief snapshot of relational frame theory (RFT), ACT, and each of its six core therapeutic processes. Chapter 2, Bypassing the Traps of Language with Experiential Practice, uses the principles suggested by RFT to provide a detailed discussion of how metaphors and exercises can enhance experiential learning and psychological flexibility. In addition, it provides instruction in the development of novel, ACT-consistent metaphors that can be tailored to specific client needs.

Chapters 3 through 8 each cover one of the six core concepts of ACT: acceptance and willingness, cognitive defusion, present-moment awareness, self-as-context, values, and committed action. Each chapter begins with a summary of the concept covered, followed by exercises and metaphors demonstrating that concept, usually with scripts for presenting the exercise or metaphor. Some exercises might be especially salient for specific types of clients (e.g., groups, trauma survivors, athletes), and many of the exercises can be tailored to be more relevant to a particular client. In these cases, we mention this in the introduction to the exercise or metaphor. Some of the exercises and metaphors come from previously published materials, and in these cases, we provide citations with page numbers. However, most of the exercises and metaphors were provided by members of the ACT community; for these, we've noted the creator's name and the year the metaphor or exercise was created or submitted to us.

Not surprisingly, chapter 9, Bringing It All Together, pulls everything together. It reviews and summarizes the role of metaphors and experiential exercises in ACT. In addition, it provides general guidelines for situating metaphors and exercises in the course of therapy, along with common pitfalls to be aware of. We also give an example of a metaphor that addresses multiple core processes.

Finally, in addition to providing worksheets, the appendices include a selected list of previously published metaphors and exercises, focusing primarily on classics that are frequently associated with ACT. At the end of the book, you'll also find a selected list of additional ACT resources. Because this book is primarily a compendium of metaphors and exercises and not a detailed ACT protocol, we recommend that this book be used as an adjunct to other, more comprehensive ACT resources.

We hope you enjoy this book as much as we enjoyed putting it together. One of the greatest advantages of ACT is its flexibility and the space it allows for creativity. We hope our book inspires you to get creative!

CHAPTER 1

OVERVIEW OF ACT

Theoretically, ACT is grounded in the experimental work of RFT, which asserts that much of human suffering is attributable to the bidirectional and generally evaluative nature of human language (Hayes, Barnes-Holmes, & Roche, 2001). Here's a quick example of how language alters our experience of the world: Nonhuman animals and young children are able to recognize that a dime is smaller than a nickel based on physical comparisons, but as we develop more complex language and cognitive functioning, these relationships can be transformed, actually changing how we relate to our experience of these objects. For instance, it is only through the acquisition of language and an understanding of socially constructed definitions that we come to relate to the comparison of a nickel and a dime in the context of monetary value and conclude that a dime is "bigger" then a nickel (Hayes et al., 2001). As far as we know, humans are the only species that engages in the behavior of relating two stimuli not only by physical properties but also, and largely, by social contingencies and conventions that are created by language (Hayes et al., 2001).

Language and Suffering

RFT also suggests that the unique capability of humans to respond to derived relationships (which places us at the top of the food chain) is exactly what traps us in emotional suffering. Specifically, our abilities to plan, predict, evaluate, verbally communicate, and relate events and stimuli to one another both help and hurt us (Hayes et al., 1999). Clearly our higher cognitive abilities allow us to solve problems. For example, if you get a terrible haircut, you can go back to your stylist (or perhaps decide to see a new stylist) and get a different haircut. If you don't like the color you just painted your walls, you can choose a new one and repaint them. At the same time, we often wrongfully try to apply these same skills to our inner experiences. We believe we should be able to control the way we think and feel in the same way we can control our hair and our houses. However, mounting research has demonstrated that the more we attempt to suppress thoughts and feelings, the more present they become (Abramowitz, Tolin, & Street, 2001; Campbell-Sills, Barlow, Brown, & Hofmann, 2006). In addition, although these attempts to avoid our internal experiences (i.e., experiential avoidance) may appear to work in the short term, they ultimately lead to a more restricted existence. For example, a person who feels anxiety every time he enters a social situation may temporarily reduce his anxiety by avoiding interpersonal encounters; however, his ability to live life freely will become greatly limited, and his fear of social interactions will persist. Thus, the verbal rules we successfully use to solve many problems in the external world typically cause suffering when we attempt to use them to "solve" painful thoughts and feelings.

ACT stipulates that overidentification with literal language leads to psychological inflexibility, and that this inflexibility is at the core of human suffering. This interrelationship can be further broken down into six core pathological processes, illustrated in figure 1.1: experiential avoidance, cognitive fusion, dominance of the conceptualized past and feared future, attachment to a conceptualized self, lack of clarity regarding values, and lack of actions directed toward values. The ACT path to emotional well-being involves moving toward psychological flexibility via six dialectical therapeutic processes.

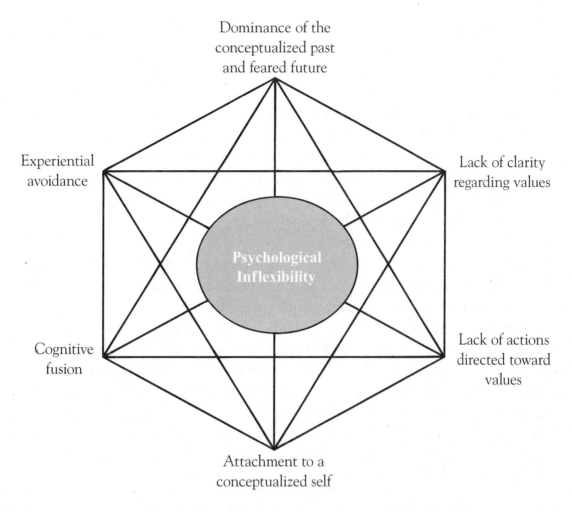

Figure 1.1. The ACT hexaflex: psychological inflexibility

ACT's Six Core Therapeutic Processes

ACT purports that psychological flexibility is at the heart of healthy emotional functioning. Through six core therapeutic processes—acceptance and willingness, cognitive defusion, present-moment awareness, self-as-context, values, and committed action—clients are guided to open up to and act upon actual experience rather than what the mind or body demands.

Acceptance

Acceptance (along with the related concept of willingness) involves making full contact with internal experiences without attempting to escape, change, or control those events. Acceptance does not imply liking or wanting, nor does it represent giving up, giving in, or resignation. Simply put, acceptance means gently holding whatever arises. At first, clients often balk at this seemingly counterintuitive idea, wondering why they would ever choose to accept emotional or physical pain. ACT suggests two reasons: because struggling to avoid pain is ineffective and often amplifies suffering, and because acceptance often facilitates taking actions in the service of living a valued life.

Consider a client who uses alcohol to numb unwanted emotions. While this may "work" in an immediate way, alcohol typically intensifies negative emotional experiences over the long run. In addition, alcohol use probably interferes with the client being the man he truly wants to be, perhaps a good friend, loving father, dedicated employee, or concerned citizen. Acceptance of unwanted emotions, on the other hand, allows the client to observe and embrace his emotional experience, uncomfortable as it may be, in the service of making alternative, valued choices, perhaps attending his son's ball game instead of heading to the bar.

Cognitive Defusion

In ACT, cognitive defusion refers to the process of stepping back from thoughts and observing their presence. ACT purports that thoughts aren't inherently problematic unless we become fused with their content and meaning (in other words, we buy what our minds are telling us) and react, often impulsively, in response. When we defuse, we disentangle from our self-talk and merely observe thoughts as entities separate from ourselves, as simply words. Cognitive defusion is the process by which we change our relationship with the content of our thoughts.

Perhaps you can relate to having a thought like *I'll never be a great therapist*. Consider the ways in which believing this thought may impact your behavior. Perhaps you'd stop putting forth your best effort or you'd turn down opportunities for continued learning. You might even give up pursuing your career or studies in psychology altogether. Fusion with this thought can come at quite a cost! Consider instead simply witnessing what your mind has just told you, in much the same way as you might watch an airplane pulling a banner across the sky. Imagine how your behavior might change (or not be affected in the first place) if you chose to simply observe the process of your mind generating this thought. This brings to light the ultimate purpose of defusion: Like acceptance, defusion creates wiggle room to make valued choices. In other words, if buying the thought *I'll never be a great therapist* causes you to change careers, simply observing that thought gives you the space to make a different choice. This doesn't mean the thought disappears; it simply means that you're no longer driven by its content. Instead, you're freed to continue moving in the directions that are most important to you, like being the best therapist you can be.

Present-Moment Awareness

Present-moment awareness has been described as one aspect of mindfulness, and as such it has been practiced for thousand of years. It can be defined as a process of nonjudgmental, present-focused awareness and therefore has direct relevance to acceptance, defusion, and self-as-context. The human mind spends a lot of time worrying about the future and ruminating about the past. While these processes may be adaptive in some ways (e.g., remembering a past mistake may prevent it from happening in the future), being dominated by thoughts of the past and future can also come at a cost. For example, focusing on past experiences may prevent current movement in valued directions.

Consider a woman who values her career and has a disappointing job interview. A continued focus on this past event may prevent her from pursuing important career goals. Focusing instead on compassionate observation of internal and external stimuli in the present moment would allow her to turn off her autopilot and respond in a more flexible, nonreactive way that's consistent with her values.

Self-as-Context

Self-as-context refers to a sense of self that transcends the content of one's experiences. In other words, there is a "you" that is observing and experiencing your inner and outer world and is also distinct from your thoughts, feelings, physical sensations, and roles. From this perspective, you are not your thoughts and feelings; rather, you are the context or arena in which they unfold. When we're stuck viewing ourselves from a *self-as-content* perspective, on the other hand, we tend to be driven by the scripts we have about ourselves, our lives, and our histories. For example, a client may have a story about himself that goes something like this: "I am the son of a firefighter. I am the grandson of a firefighter. Good firefighters are brave. Brave firefighters don't show their feelings. I must become a good firefighter." If the client defines his identity by the content of his story, it will drive his actions—even if those actions aren't consistent with his personal values. Self-as-context aims to shift the client from this perspective to one of observer and experiencer of life as it unfolds. He may then choose his actions based on his values, rather than based on the stories he has about himself and his roles.

Values

In ACT, values are paths or directions defined by the individual as important and meaningful. Values define who we truly want to be and what we want to stand for. Traveling in valued directions makes life rich and fulfilling. ACT isn't about changing internal private events; it's about changing behaviors. Values provide the road map for making these changes. For example, if one of your values is having intimate and trusting relationships, you may behave in accord with that by calling your partner to say "I love you" or making time to talk with a friend about her day. A key feature of values is that they cannot be permanently achieved. Another feature is that values are personal: what is important to one person may not be important to another, and what is valued by an individual's parents or culture may not be important to that person. To facilitate making this distinction, you might ask yourself, "If no one knew I was doing this, would it still be important to me?" Acceptance, defusion, present-moment awareness, and self-as-context are practiced to promote greater flexibility in the service of living in accordance with personal values.

Committed Action

Finally, committed action is simply walking the walk. Values provide the direction, and committed action is the actual behavior change. You might help clients identify committed actions by talking about goals that are in line with their identified values. It's important to clarify the difference between values and goals. A value may be thought of as a direction or path that is never finished, achieved, or accomplished, whereas a goal can be checked off a to-do list when it has been completed. For example, you may value learning, education, and helping others, so you set a goal to get an advanced degree in a mental-health field. Learning and helping are ongoing, while getting a degree has an end point. It is in the actual practice of taking committed actions that ACT may begin to resemble traditional behavior therapy. ACT therapists may use problem-solving strategies, exposure techniques, assertive communication skills, and the like in an effort to get clients moving in valued directions. Of course, internal obstacles, such as thoughts and feelings, will arise and threaten to interfere with taking actions in line with those values. Thus, acceptance, defusion, present-moment awareness, and self-as-context are practiced in the service of overcoming those obstacles.

Psychological Flexibility

To sum up, the ultimate goal in ACT is psychological flexibility (illustrated in figure 1.2), which is the ability to be fully present and open to our experiences so that we can take actions guided by our values. More simply put, psychological flexibility is the ability to be present, open up, and do what matters (Harris, 2009). Ultimately, being present, opening up, and doing what matters leads to a life that's rich, meaningful, and characterized by true vitality.

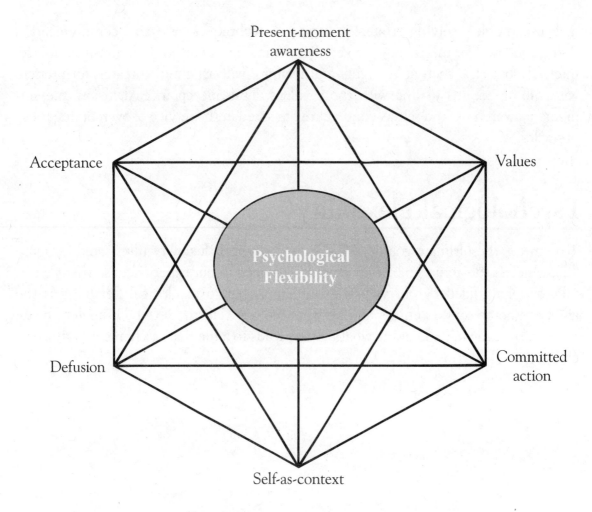

Figure 1.2. The ACT hexaflex: psychological flexibility

CHAPTER 2

BYPASSING THE TRAPS OF LANGUAGE WITH EXPERIENTIAL PRACTICE

Matthieu Villatte, Jennifer L. Villatte, and Jean-Louis Monestès

When confronted with the tricks that language plays on people who suffer from psychological difficulties (and people in general, us included), therapists need to reconnect clients to useful elements of their experience. In psychotherapy, this cannot be done without language, since almost everything that happens in a therapy session is made of symbolic interactions. (Even a moment of silence often means something!) Thus, therapists need to use language in an experiential way, and this is the path chosen by ACT and other third-wave psychotherapies, such as mindfulness-based cognitive therapy (Segal, Williams, & Teasdale, 2002), dialectical behavior therapy (Linehan, 1993a), and functional analytic psychotherapy (Kohlenberg & Tsai, 1991).

In RFT terms, our aim as experiential therapists is to undermine the arbitrary application of language when it leads to ineffective behaviors, and to use language to increase contact with nonarbitrary features of the environment. This process is initiated as soon as therapy begins, as you conduct a functional assessment of the client's problematic behaviors. For example, you can ask questions such as these:

- *When you wait to feel less depressed before going back to work, what happens?*

THE BIG BOOK OF ACT METAPHORS

- *How has the strategy you're following to deal with your depressed feelings worked so far?*

- *When you don't admit that you're wrong, does it make you feel closer or farther away from the person you're arguing with?*

Note that, while language is obviously employed to ask these questions, they are intended to direct clients' attention to what they concretely experience in life. This is significantly different from the process that would be targeted by a question such as "Do you think that admitting you're wrong is truly a sign of weakness?" This type of question prompts clients to evaluate the credibility of the statement without consideration for their experience. As a result, they're likely to think that the statement is true no matter what happens in their life.

Different Kinds of Experiential Practice

A wide range of experiential techniques can be used throughout the course of ACT therapy. Mindfulness constitutes one of the most well-known and empirically supported sets of exercises employed in therapies that emphasize contact with experience over changing thoughts (Hayes, Villatte, Levin, & Hildebrandt, 2011). Typical mindfulness techniques consist of a variety of meditation exercises in which clients are trained to observe every perceivable event, both external, such as sounds and smells, and internal, such as thoughts and sensations. From an RFT perspective, this is done to increase attention to nonarbitrary aspects of the environment, including the mental environment. Metaphorically, we can say that this process widens the holes of the filter created by language, letting in more direct experience. For example, when clients observe their bodily sensations for a long period of time, as in a body-scan exercise (Kabat-Zinn, 1991), they are encouraged to notice and allow the full range of intrinsic features of these sensations and to let go of judgments and evaluations produced by language. More concretely, if a client feels pain in his arm, he is encouraged to observe the multiple facets of this sensation (e.g., Does it burn? Does it throb? Is it acute or diffused?), while reactions or judgments (e.g., "It's unbearable" or "I hate feeling this sensation") are weakened by instructions to "let go."

Interestingly, even verbal forms of control can help decrease certain sources of verbal control, as in the instruction "Let go of judgments." From an RFT view, this isn't paradoxical, as verbal control per se is only problematic when the insensitivity it generates leads to ineffective behaviors. If clients are encouraged to observe the course of their thoughts without reacting to them, their behavior is indeed controlled by a rule, but a rule that increases the likelihood that they will adopt new behaviors more adapted to their environment.

In ACT, mindfulness is considered to be a combination of processes, including acceptance, defusion, contact with the present moment, and self-as-context (Wilson & DuFrene, 2009). Each of these processes can be targeted with relatively specific techniques, even if interactions between the processes are quite common (Hayes, Strosahl, & Wilson, 2011). For example, a client may be encouraged to "make room for a painful emotion" after the evocation of a difficult memory. In RFT terms, the therapist creates a verbal context that triggers a painful psychological event and encourages the client to contact the consequences of not trying to escape it. While the client may originally think that painful emotions ought to be avoided, directly experiencing acceptance may expand the range of her future reactions to painful emotions and make certain actions more available (e.g., accepting the feeling of anxiety in order to be able to speak in public, or accepting feeling depressed in order to be able to do meaningful activities again).

Defusion exercises often consist of recontacting the nonarbitrary characteristics of verbal stimuli. For example, repeating a word very quickly for thirty to forty seconds decreases the meaning carried by an originally nonarbitrary sequence of sounds. In more general terms, the client is led to perceive that a word is just a word and not the actual event it refers to. Hence, reactions to words evoking danger (e.g., "death") or fostering rigidity (e.g., "I have to") can become more flexible.

Exercises focusing on the present moment, for example, consist of directing attention to breathing. Since breathing always takes place in the present, this helps clients undermine the control exerted by language when it takes them to the past or to the future, away from present sources of satisfaction or actual consequences of their behavior.

Self-as-context exercises target a specific kind of verbal skills (perspective taking) and often involve observing oneself from another point of view through imagination. This puts clients in contact with the distinction between fleeting descriptions of the self and a more permanent perception based on a continuous perspective.

Interestingly, some experiential exercises in ACT aim at *increasing* verbal control over direct contingencies. In this case, the goal is to elaborate a network of verbal relations establishing a connection between a discrete event or action and meaningful but distant or abstract consequences. For example, clients may be asked to set an alarm randomly, notice what they're doing each time the alarm sounds, and observe whether that action is connected to a value in an important domain of life. For example, if the alarm sounds in the middle of a conversation with a friend, a client might notice that this action is in a relation of hierarchy with his value for connection in relationships—talking with a friend is part of what he does to be close to his friends. (In RFT terms, talking with a friend is in a relation of hierarchy with "connection in relationships" because this higher-order concept includes a broad set of possible actions, such as lending a hand to a friend who needs help, inviting a friend for dinner, or sharing personal experience with a friend.)

Such exercises can be helpful for clients who have difficulties connecting with what makes their actions meaningful in the moment, especially if the consequences of these actions are abstract and may never be directly contacted. For example, making time for her children might be aversive for a parent who is devoted to her work, but she can establish a relation of hierarchy between being there for her children and the abstract concept of "being a good parent." She can also establish an if-then relationship between "if I raise my children well" and the distant consequence that she may never actually contact: "they will have a happy adult life." As a consequence of such increased awareness, the client might be more able to engage in concrete actions directed toward her values, strengthening the probability that these actions will remain in her behavioral repertoire. This is particularly useful when engaging in valued actions brings about painful emotions. For example, while expressing one's feelings to a partner may enhance intimacy, it may also trigger anxiety. In this case, verbally connecting with what matters (intimacy with one's partner) can change the meaning of the immediate aversive experience: feeling anxious becomes a sign that one is moving toward intimacy.

Metaphor as an Example of the Experiential Use of Language

Formal experiential exercises aren't the only way you can help clients undermine the negative effects of language. For example, you can also point clients' attention toward their direct experience simply by means of questions, reformulations, and prompts to adopt a different perspective. Furthermore, certain forms of language are themselves genuine experiential triggers. In particular, metaphors are emblematic of the experiential use of language in ACT, which employs this tool for a specific purpose. Metaphors make abstract concepts concrete by providing a rich verbal context that evokes thoughts, feelings, and behaviors similar to those evoked by the client's actual situation.

The story-like quality of metaphors has the advantage of providing instructive lessons that are rich in emotional and perceptual detail, mimicking direct contact with the environment and making the experience more memorable. Metaphors create a verbal world where clients can explore new behaviors and discover the contingencies for themselves, circumventing the potential traps of learning by rules. Metaphors also draw attention to salient features of a situation that may go unnoticed in clients' real-world environment, thus liberating them from the cage built by language. Here again, RFT provides guiding principles for building metaphors that have maximal therapeutic impact.

Relation of Relations

As discussed in chapter 1, from an RFT point of view language is made of relations among things. We build and understand relations, and we respond to these relations. In some cases, a simple relation between two events can influence our behavior. For example, if a waitress brings a dish to our table and says, "It's very hot!" we will probably be careful when touching the plate. We understand the relation built by the waitress between the plate and "hot," and this influences the way we interact with the plate. In other cases, a combination of simple relations can govern behaviors in a more sophisticated way, as when following complex instructions (O'Hora, Barnes-Holmes, Roche, & Smeets, 2004).

Sometimes a relation can be established between two sets of relations and trigger interesting reactions, and this is often the case with metaphors (Lipkens & Hayes, 2009; Stewart, Barnes-Holmes, Hayes, & Lipkens, 2001). Consider the example of a man telling his beloved partner that she is the compass of his life. This is obviously a metaphor, since the woman isn't actually a compass. There is, however, a similarity between what the woman and a compass bring to the man. If the man follows his partner's advice, he'll find his way in life, and if he follows the compass's directions, he'll find his way in the forest. In RFT terms, a relation of equivalence links two sets of conditional relations (see figure 2.1). The man could also tell his partner that if she took the afternoon off work and spent it with him, this would light up his day. Once again, the woman is obviously not going to actually bring more light to the man. However, bringing joy by spending the afternoon with him is similar to the sun literally bringing light to his day. Again, in RFT terms, a relation of equivalence links these two sets of conditional relations. If the woman spends the afternoon with her partner, she will bring him joy, and if the sun emerges from behind clouds, it will bring light.

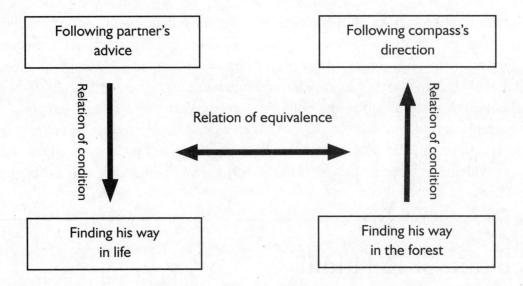

Figure 2.1. A relation of equivalence between two sets of conditional relations

Highlighting the Function of Behavior Through Metaphor

Metaphors employed in ACT are often more elaborate than the preceding examples, but they lean on the same principle. For example, the classic Hungry Tiger metaphor (Hayes, 2005, pp. 36–37) consists of asking a client to imagine finding a baby tiger in front of her door and having to take care of it until a shelter is found. As days pass, the tiger begins growling with hunger, so the client gives him some food, but the tiger gets stronger as a result, and when he gets hungry again, he becomes very aggressive. The client has no choice but to give more food to the tiger, which makes him even stronger and more aggressive when hungry, creating a vicious circle. This metaphor is presented to the client to draw a parallel with counterproductive attempts to suppress painful emotions.

As in the examples above, a relation of equivalence also exists between two conditional relations here: "If I feed the tiger to calm him down, the tiger will get stronger and more aggressive, and if I try to suppress my painful emotions, the emotions will get stronger and more difficult to bear." Yet clients often consider avoidance to be the best strategy for alleviating suffering, probably because of the short-term relief often afforded by emotional suppression and because of the insensitivity generated by following rules, in this case "I need to think of something else so I can feel better." You can use such a metaphor to direct the client's attention to the concrete consequences of her actions in a context that's topographically different from her problematic situation but that contains a similar functional sequence. If the client perceives the functional equivalence between the two situations, she may see her own emotional suppression as counterproductive in the long-term, creating an opportunity for behavior change.

There are numerous metaphors created by the community of ACT therapists (many of which are in this book), in a variety of languages and cultures, targeting different processes, and using different forms. In some cases, the metaphor has the form of a concrete exercise requiring clients to take action and observe the consequences of different strategies. For example, the Blind Writing exercise (which appears in Monestès & Villatte, 2011, p. 49) consists of asking the client to write a sentence on a board while the therapist puts a visual obstacle in front of his eyes. In the first phase, the client is asked to do everything he can to be able to see while writing, which leads to spending all his energy on avoiding the obstacle rather than on writing. In the second phase, he's asked to try another approach: instead of attempting to get rid of the obstacle, he's asked to focus his efforts on writing even if he can't see the board. With this approach, the client is generally able to write a legible sentence—without the frustration and wasted energy of struggling with the obstacle. A relationship is thus established between trying to get rid of painful emotions and trying to get rid of the visual obstacle. In both contexts, attempts to remove the obstacle monopolize the client's efforts and detract from the goal at hand, whereas accepting the presence of difficulties (painful emotions or the visual obstacle) allows the client to engage in the desired action with success. In this physical metaphor, as in metaphors presented as stories, the ultimate goal is to transform the function of the problematic behavior so that ineffective strategies can be seen for what they are, allowing new behaviors that better fit the environment to emerge.

Building a Therapeutic Metaphor

Based on the elements we've presented in this chapter, you can see that two main principles are key in building an efficient, novel metaphor in therapy. First, as noted earlier, it's crucial that clients be able to observe the concrete consequences of their actions in the situation presented in the metaphor (e.g., feeding the tiger has the consequence of making the tiger bigger, stronger, and more demanding). While a metaphor like the Hungry Tiger is easily understood by most clients, it has the limitation of leaning on a situation that most people will never encounter. Thus, it requires another level of relational activity: imagining what would happen if one were to feed a hungry baby tiger.

In another example that targets the counterproductiveness of avoidance, the Quicksand metaphor (Hayes, 2005, pp. 3–4), clients probably haven't experienced that situation either. However, it is very possible that they have at least seen a representation of someone sinking in quicksand in a movie, which is less likely for finding a tiger at the front door. In the case of struggling in quicksand, we can assume that observing the consequences of the behavior of struggling is a bit easier for clients because of this familiarity, if not from experience, at least from seeing it in a movie. An even better approach is to build metaphors on the personal history and cultural background of individual clients. This ensures that clients will have a direct, concrete knowledge of what happens after they execute a given action. Such metaphors can be built using references to people, objects, and events that are familiar to clients or using personal experiences they've previously reported.

The second main principle for building therapeutic metaphors is that the function of events in the metaphor must match the function of events salient to the clinical situation. The application of metaphors and exercises can get confusing if you don't pay careful attention to the context (i.e., the specific ACT process) for which they're used. For example, while metaphors like the Hungry Tiger and Quicksand are almost universally categorized as metaphors building acceptance, they might have this effect only if the context in which they're used involves avoidance primarily. Imagine a situation in which a client displays difficulties with staying engaged in an action that could bring satisfaction in the long term. Using the Hungry Tiger might work well if the client tends to give up easily as a result of experiential avoidance (e.g., escaping the anxiety that shows up when engaging in an activity). Indeed, such a client who is told that story might perceive that trying to get rid of a painful emotion by disengaging from the activity will make the emotion worse (e.g., he might feel sad and guilty for having quit the activity). However, if the reason for disengaging from the activity is a lack of perceived connection between this activity and distant or abstract consequences (i.e., his values), then using a metaphor that emphasizes the deleterious effects of persistence probably isn't the most appropriate move. In this case, a metaphor focused on travel or steps along a journey may be a more efficient tool, as it offers a comparison for discrete actions directed toward values; in this case, both the metaphor and the client's situation and present actions are linked to distant or abstract consequences.

In addition to ensuring a functional match between the metaphor and the clinical situation, getting close to a topographical match can be useful in the early stages of therapy, as a formal resemblance may facilitate the perception of equivalence. For example, if a client demonstrates behaviors that are functionally avoidant and topographically passive (e.g., not speaking in public to avoid anxiety), then a metaphor including a passive behavior will be more appropriate (e.g., stopping driving in the presence of fog, explored in clinical vignettes later in this chapter). This wouldn't be the case with the Hungry Tiger and Quicksand metaphors, since the topography of avoidance behavior in these metaphors is active (i.e., persistent feeding and struggling). Progressively, the therapist can introduce metaphors that are functionally similar but topographically more varied to generalize to a variety of the client's problematic behaviors. Using the same example, this could be particularly useful if the client avoids anxiety by not speaking in public and by drinking alcohol. Indeed, these two behaviors are functionally similar since they both aim at suppressing anxiety, but they're topographically different since one is passive and the other is active.

To summarize, to build an effective therapeutic metaphor, you first need to conduct a precise functional analysis of the client's difficulties to ensure accurate targeting of the relevant ACT processes. Using the client's cultural background or personal experience will help the client observe the relationship between the metaphor and his own situation. Likewise, creating a functional match between the metaphor and the client's situation will facilitate the client's understanding of the similarities between the consequences observed in the metaphor and his own situation. In addition, elements such as topographical similarities that can help the client perceive the connections between his personal situation and the metaphor should be considered when building the metaphor.

Delivering Experiential Metaphors

The way a metaphor is delivered is key in helping clients perceive the concrete consequences of their actions through the connection between the metaphor and their own situation. In particular, it's useful to emphasize an experiential presentation of the metaphor, which makes interaction with the elements of the story more concrete, emotionally evocative, and memorable. To do so, the therapist would use the present indicative tense rather than the conditional form, encouraging the client to observe the situation as if it were really happening in the here and now. Concretely, this means the therapist would say, "You walk in the desert and, suddenly, you step in quicksand. What do you do now?" rather than, "Imagine that you were in the desert and you stepped in quicksand. What would you do then?"

In addition, you can direct the client's attention toward her own current reactions to the story as it unfolds. For example, the therapist may ask, "What happens as you try to escape the quicksand?" "How do you feel now?" or "What are the thoughts that come to your mind as you keep sinking?" Although you can use contextual cues to directly establish the perception of equivalence between the metaphor and the clinical situation, such directive moves should typically be limited. For instance, it's preferable to avoid saying, "Struggling with quicksand *is like* struggling with anxiety," because doing so leads the client to learn through rules rather than direct experience. While these two forms of learning are never totally separated in humans, using excessively directive rules misses the opportunity to increase influence by direct consequences. Instead, you can strengthen direct perception by mixing the vocabulary between the metaphorical and actual situations. For example, after exploring the Quicksand story for a while, you might say, "And what do you do when you start sinking in your anxiety?" Likewise, with the Hungry Tiger metaphor, you might say, "What happens when your anxiety starts to get hungry and makes aggressive demands?"

Clinical Examples

The following clinical vignettes exemplify two alternative ways of delivering a metaphor. We begin with an introduction that covers ground common to both approaches. Next, we show a very directive presentation of the metaphor. The final section emphasizes an experiential delivery based on RFT principles. We present the didactic version first and then demonstrate how it can be developed in an experiential presentation.

Introduction

Therapist: So it's very difficult for you to go out to see your friends and family, and you said that even going to work is becoming really burdensome. What are the thoughts that come to your mind when a friend invites you to go out, for example?

Client: I feel so depressed that I don't even know what I want. Even when I think I want to go, I'm afraid I'm going to be bored or too tired.... I feel lost.

Therapist: And then you decide to decline the invitation?

Client: Yeah. I feel so uncertain that I just end up staying at home.

Therapist: So it looks like these thoughts are preventing you from going out with your friends. Is that right?

Client: I guess we can say that.

Didactic Version

Therapist: It sounds like, when you're having these thoughts and are uncertain about what you want, it's as if you were driving in a dense fog that prevented you from seeing the road well. It's so difficult to see where you're going in the fog, so you stop the car and wait until it goes away. What do you think?

The therapist has established a connection between the client's situation and driving in the fog by using the explicit contextual cue "it's as if." Additionally, the therapist chose the context of driving in the fog because it is indeed a foggy day and the client drove to the session in the fog.

Client: I guess it's true that I'm not moving forward anymore.

Therapist: But when you drive and there's fog on the road, do you actually stop until it goes away?

The therapist initiated the connection between the function of not going out in the presence of thoughts and feelings that serve as barriers by pointing to the fact that the client would actually act differently in a similar situation.

Client: Well, no, because you never know how long it would take. I might drive more slowly and carefully, but I keep going.

Therapist: And sometimes it doesn't even go away, right? You reach your destination and there's still fog on the road...

Client: Yes, it can happen.

Therapist: It looks like what you're doing with your thoughts.... When you think that you'll be too tired to go out, for example, it's as if you were doing the opposite of what you would do when you drive in the fog.

The therapist again used an explicit contextual cue ("it's as if you were doing the opposite") to establish a relation of opposition between what the client does in the fog and what he does in the presence of thoughts and feelings that serve as barriers. The aim of this explicit reformulation is to strengthen the relation between the client's situation and the situation contained in the metaphor, and at the same time show the differing effects of the two alternative behaviors.

Client: I guess that's true. I wait for it to get better instead of moving forward.

Experiential Version

Therapist: You know that I often use exercises in our sessions, right?

Client: Yes.

Therapist: Would you be okay with following me on another one?

Client: Yes, okay.

Therapist: Did you notice fog on the road today?

The therapist has brought the client's attention to his personal experience in order to help him observe the concrete elements of the situation.

Client: Yeah, it was hard to see on my way here.

Therapist: How did you feel this morning when you saw the fog?

The therapist has brought the client's attention to his thoughts and feelings.

Client: Well, kind of annoyed that I had to go out. It's really not easy to drive when it's like that.

Therapist: Try to remember when you were on the road and it was hard to see. Just imagine that you are still there.... How do you feel?

The therapist is using the present indicative tense to bring the metaphor into the here and now and have the client describe his current thoughts, sensations, and emotions. This is meant to help the client observe the sequence of events as in a formal functional assessment, but in a way that makes the concrete features of the experience more salient.

Client:	I feel kind of stuck…
Therapist:	What kind of sensations does that bring in your body?
Client:	The muscles in my neck are tensed…. My eyes hurt because it's hard to see the road with the fog.
Therapist:	And what do you think at this very moment?
Client:	I think I'd be better in my bed.
Therapist:	And what do you do?
Client:	Well, I keep driving anyway because I have my appointment with you.
Therapist:	Does the fog affect your driving, though?
Client:	I have to drive slowly. I was hoping it would get better, but it never went away. The fog is still here.

At this point, the relations included in the metaphor are clearly established. The fog makes it hard to drive, but stopping driving would prevent the client from reaching his destination. Thus, keeping driving even if doing so requires more caution seems to be more adaptive. Note that the therapist only asked about the client's personal experience and never provided any of the answers. The last question oriented the client toward the difficulty of driving in the fog, which will be useful later for validating the difficulty of acting in the presence of thoughts and feelings that serve as barriers.

Therapist:	When I hear you talk about what happens when a friend invites you to go out, I feel like a fog rises all around you.

The therapist has begun mixing the vocabulary of the two situations to suggest equivalence between the two situations.

Client:	When I stay at home?

Once you start mixing the vocabulary of the two verbal networks, the client can either get a little confused at first or understand immediately the correspondence between the two situations. You must be prepared to adapt to either reaction. In the current case, the therapist returns to the functional assessment of the original situation and then starts mixing the vocabulary again.

Therapist:	Why do you stay at home?

Client: Because I'm too depressed. I don't know what I want.

Therapist: So you stop driving?

Mixing the vocabulary of driving in the fog and going out makes the paradox of acting differently in two similar situations even more salient. On the one hand, the client chooses to keep moving forward in the fog, and on the other, he chooses to stop in the presence of difficult thoughts and feelings.

Client: I didn't think about it that way, but yeah… I guess I stop driving, like you say.

Therapist: These thoughts that you're too depressed, that you don't know what you want… Are you saying that they're too thick to drive through?

The therapist is asking the client if he relates the influence of barriers to going out and the influence of the fog on driving according to a relation of comparison. In other words, does the client consider barrier thoughts to have a stronger impact than the fog? Mixing the vocabulary helps the client perceive the limitations of acting based on such a way of thinking.

Client: I guess that's what I think in the moment.

The client has recognized that, for him, difficult thoughts and feelings have a greater impact than the fog. However, adding "in the moment" indicates that he's entering the early stages of distancing from this way of thinking.

Therapist: When you're on the road and these thoughts of feeling depressed and uncertain get so thick that you have a hard time seeing the road, could you imagine that you might keep driving anyway?

The therapist has suggested an alternative behavior while still mixing the vocabulary of the two situations to make the efficiency of this new behavior more salient.

Client: Like I kept driving to come here today?

Therapist: You said you didn't feel like doing that either, right?

By saying "either," the therapist used a contextual cue aimed at strengthening the equivalence between driving in spite of the fog and going out in spite of feeling depressed, thus reinforcing the function of the alternative behavior. In this way, the behavior may become appropriate in the eyes of the client.

Client: I would have preferred staying in bed.

Therapist: And yet you're here. And the fog is still here too.

The therapist has directly established a relationship between driving in the presence of fog with the purpose of indirectly establishing a similar relation between taking valued action in the presence of thoughts and feelings that function as barriers, following the principle of defusion in ACT.

Client: Yes, that's true. I am here in spite of the fog.

The experiential version of the dialogue highlights principles that are consistent with what RFT tells us about the effects of language processes. These are ideal principles; however, we don't propose them as absolute and rigid rules for delivering effective metaphors. They should therefore be used flexibly, with acute attention to the function of the chosen therapeutic moves and with workability as the main criterion for evaluating those moves.

Summary

In this chapter, we provided a framework for understanding how metaphors work, how to build them, and how to use them in therapy. While research will certainly expand the knowledge of language processes involved in psychopathology and therapy, clinicians already have at their disposal a set of principles based on RFT that they can apply concretely and with flexibility. The metaphor of driving a car is sometimes used to talk about the connection between RFT and how therapists conduct ACT therapy: perhaps the driver doesn't need to understand how the car functions to drive it well. In this view, knowledge of RFT isn't necessary for an effective clinical practice. However, the metaphor can also be interpreted slightly differently. If you consider that doing ACT requires the skills of a race car driver, then it's useful to look under the hood of the car and learn some basic principles about how it functions. We believe that the use of metaphors and exercises in therapy constitutes an example in which drivers can improve their skills by increasing their knowledge of language processes. We hope that further development of RFT principles will even further expand the ways clinical practice can be directly nurtured by those principles.

CHAPTER 3

ACCEPTANCE AND WILLINGNESS

with Pia S. Heppner

The concepts of acceptance and willingness stand in contrast to experiential avoidance and psychological inflexibility. Acceptance involves the action of allowing the presence of all experiences—internal and external, positive and negative—as they are in the moment, without attempting to change the form or frequency of these experiences. Thus, the behavior of acceptance is an alternative to experiential avoidance. Willingness is a closely related behavior of taking an open and aware stance that can facilitate acceptance. This stance doesn't mean believing our thoughts to be true (e.g., *I'm a failure*), nor does it mean resignation. Rather, it is an experiential recognition that many experiences include elements that simply cannot be changed, such as spontaneous emotions, memories, external stressors, and other people's choices or behaviors (Robinson & Strosahl, 2008). Whereas attempts to get rid of, avoid, or control these experiences can limit our choices and lead to psychological inflexibility, acceptance and willingness allow us to experience whatever is present when doing so would foster values-based action.

Control as the Problem

As an initial step toward fostering acceptance and willingness, understanding a client's unworkable control agenda is central to ACT case conceptualization. Given the ability of human beings to get trapped by the content of language and our evolutionary history, it's easy to get pulled into the agenda of eliminating psychological (or physical) pain even in domains that are beyond the scope of our control. Buying into the possibility that pain can be dealt with and should be eliminated can cause clients to become stuck in a mode of control. In early stages of therapy, it's useful to explore attempts at control with exercises such as compiling a Suffering Inventory (Hayes, 2005, pp. 12–13) and posing the "magic wand" question (Hayes, 2005, pp. 14). The Suffering Inventory gives the client an opportunity to outline all of the thoughts, feelings, memories, urges, bodily sensations, and other private events that generate difficult and persistent negative reactions. The "magic wand" question asks what the client's life would be like if everything on the suffering inventory magically vanished. Together, these approaches help elucidate which painful experiences the client would wish away, providing useful insight into her unworkable control agenda. In further examining this agenda, it's important to make a distinction between "clean" pain—the natural and spontaneous emotions, memories, and other private events that show up in the context of living life—versus "dirty" pain, or suffering, which shows up in the context of efforts to control or avoid the pain that naturally occurs in life.

Once there's an understanding of the client's painful experiences, you and the client can work together to review the strategies she uses in the service of controlling or avoiding pain. This is done to help clarify both the function and the consequences of these strategies and bring to light the workability or unworkability of the underlying control agenda. New metaphors such as those found in this chapter or traditional ones such as the Man in the Hole (Hayes et al., 1999, pp. 101–104) and Quicksand (Hayes, 2005, pp. 3–4) can illustrate how efforts to control or eliminate pain (i.e., experiential avoidance) may not only be ineffective, but actually cause more problems. With these metaphors, you and the client can explore how earnest efforts to deal with difficult, unchangeable situations may result in a narrowing of options (e.g., choosing to use shovel after shovel in efforts to get out of a hole) and, ultimately, becoming more mired in the situation as efforts to escape it are increased (e.g., sinking in deeper each time she struggles to get out of the quicksand).

The Problem with Problem Solving

The distinction between attempts to control problems outside versus inside the skin is an important one in ACT. Using examples such as removing a clock from the room because you don't like it or taking your car to the shop when you begin to hear a loud noise under the hood helps illustrate the usefulness of problem solving for practical, outside-the-skin problems. In fact, this type of problem solving is so ingrained that people can launch into this mode instantaneously without even thinking of the actual steps involved in solving a problem. Reviewing the specific steps in the problem-solving process can help highlight how the steps that are meant to fix a situation might actually contribute to the pitfalls of the unworkable control agenda.

For example, take the situation of coming home and smelling gas in the kitchen. This problem can probably be fixed within a matter of seconds, but doing so could involve several steps:

1. Recognizing that something is wrong (detecting a strange odor)

2. Identifying the cause (figuring out that the odor is gas from the stove and that a knob isn't completely shut off)

3. Anticipating what could happen if things continue and no action is taken (knowing that there could be an explosion if there's a spark)

4. Determining what should be done and executing it (turning the knob off and opening windows)

5. Evaluating whether the plan worked by comparing the actual outcome to the expected outcome (waiting to see if the odor dissipates)

6. Determining what was learned and figuring out how to prevent or handle similar problems in the future (calling one's partner and sharing the experience)

In this example, each step seems to have a role in moving toward resolution of the problem. However, if these steps are applied to problems under the skin, is it possible that they could be involved in generating suffering or psychological inflexibility? For instance, step 2, identifying a cause, could be harmful if it shows up in the form of attributing blame or responsibility (e.g., "It was all my fault" or "You should have known better"). Likewise, looking into the future for potential consequences of situations and choices, as in step 3, might look like excessive worrying (e.g., "I know I need to do this, but what if _____ happens?") if it becomes a predominant mode. Step 4, determining what should be done and doing it, requires accessing verbal knowledge or a rule (e.g., a spark will cause an explosion if there's a dense concentration of flammable gas). However, when dealing with problems outside our control, trying to adhere to such rules about how things *should* be and behaving strictly based on those rules (e.g., "I'll make changes only on my terms" or "Tit for tat—that's how I see it") can maintain the position of being stuck as a person who waits for his circumstances or other people to change, and struggles against what is.

Furthermore, when the processes of evaluation, comparison, and judgment required in step 5 are applied to the self, they might contribute to a persistent view of chronically falling short of a standard and the use of negative labels about oneself (e.g., "Why can't I just stop being this way?" or "I'm a loser, and most people probably think that way about me too."). Finally, while incorporating cognitive units from experience (e.g., lessons about what worked, evaluations) into verbal knowledge, as in step 6, might help a person deal effectively with similar situations in the future, when this process is applied to the self or problems under the skin, it may come at a tremendous cost. Evaluations and labels can be incorporated into a conceptualized view of the self or the world that's harmful and limiting (e.g., "I should just stop trying," "Maybe if I stop caring, I won't get hurt again," or "That's how people are, so why should I bother getting close to anyone?").

You can conduct a similar exercise with a client by outlining the steps involved in solving an external problem from his life and then applying those steps to the problem the client is bringing into therapy. For instance, the two of you can work with an external problem where the client can readily envision a specific, desired outcome (e.g., having more financial flexibility during retirement in fifteen years). Together, you can identify factors in his current circumstances that may hinder reaching this outcome (maintaining a lifestyle that's creating more debt); brainstorm all behavioral options that will make this goal possible (making financial compromises now and saving a certain amount per month); and develop a plan to monitor progress. You can then highlight processes involved in executing these steps, such as focusing on problem areas (what isn't working well), forecasting and planning ahead, and evaluating progress along the way to see if the changes are actually beneficial.

You can then compare how the client has engaged in these same steps in "resolving" a problem under the skin (e.g., trying to improve his self-esteem through continuous efforts to prove himself to others, losing weight, or focusing on his imperfections) and explore how well these efforts have worked (e.g., by asking, "Are you finally a more confident version of your old self? If not, did you try hard enough? What if things never change for you?"). This can underscore the distinction between what works in the outside world and what works inside the skin. It can also generate an understanding of the costs of these control processes when applied to problems outside his control, and especially when applied to himself.

Experiential avoidance or efforts to control can not only create and maintain "dirty" pain and suffering but also undermine a person's ability to take helpful action. After reviewing all of the mind's suggested ways of fixing the problem that a client struggles with internally, you might ask if any of the strategies from "this fixing the problem" approach have helped the client get through his difficult experience. The answer is often a clear no, and in most cases, these strategies have only made things worse. This creates an opening to shift the focus from problem solving to acknowledging his experience openly and exploring other behavioral options for responding to difficult circumstances.

Acceptance and Willingness: Enhancing Behavioral Flexibility

The Serenity Prayer, which is firmly rooted in the 12-step recovery program, is a succinct and meaningful way of talking about acceptance and willingness when addressing difficult life circumstances. The prayer states, "Grant me the serenity to accept the things I cannot change, the courage to change the things I can, and the wisdom to know the difference." Also, and more subtly, it speaks to the premise that we have the ability to choose how to respond—whether to accept or to change—and to discern which response may be better suited to a given situation. The ultimate goal of acceptance and willingness is to increase behavioral options, developing the flexibility to respond as the situation requires. However, given the strong pull of control and the ease with which we humans can launch into problem solving, behavioral options other than control or avoidance aren't always readily apparent. Even if you can see multiple options, some clients may gravitate toward the option that's most familiar or one that helps maintain avoidance or control of painful internal experiences. Others may decide to behave differently but only under certain conditions (e.g., only if it doesn't become too difficult); as a result, encountering discomfort along the way will thwart efforts to continue in that chosen action.

Alternatively, the willingness to acknowledge and have the uncomfortable experiences that come with choosing acceptance can greatly enhance the ability to behave freely. Here's how a client with cancer described his experience of willingness: Toward the end of an ACT-based cancer support group, he was experiencing pain and ongoing digestive problems and had resumed chemotherapy. At the last group session, he shared that being willing had afforded him more options. With further probing, he explained that if he was willing to have pain and other physical symptoms, he could do what he wanted. He chose to not struggle with his physical difficulties and instead refocus his attention and efforts toward areas of living that mattered greatly to him, like parenting and helping others. This is not to say that engaging in more activities consistent with his values was easy, but at least he could shift his focus away from constant management of his physical symptoms and find a way to engage in meaningful activities.

The behavioral flexibility that comes with acceptance may also involve *not* doing. Taking a willing stance and approaching experiences with acceptance may involve recognizing and choosing the option to *not* follow an urge to change one's experience. This might be relevant for a client who's having difficulties related to impulsive behavior, for example, lashing out verbally at her partner when she feels angry. Willingly not taking action is in contrast to not taking action because of avoidance, such as not returning a phone call from a friend to avoid feeing anxiety. Brief exercises like noticing an itch and not scratching it can easily demonstrate this point and allow clients to let things be as they are in the moment, seeing what they might experience if they don't engage in attempts to control.

The stance of letting things be as they are and not engaging in behavior to change internal experiences may be particularly difficult for those who are adept at using "good" coping skills, like strategies to reduce stress or positive self-affirmations. These "positive" strategies may function as experiential avoidance, and it can be harder to see their potential costs. Further, therapists can fall into the trap of reinforcing these control strategies by going along with the positive talk. Sometimes a client might disclose something difficult and then try to move away from it, for example, by discounting or modifying the feeling or changing topics (e.g., "I'm so down and wish I could be closer to my kids. But I'm okay. I still have a good job, and I'm pretty healthy for my age."). In such moments, you might gently ask the client to pause there or turn toward what he had just shared before moving on and see if he can talk more about that feeling or situation. These instances of clients sharing something that warrants more exploration might look quite different from storytelling or presenting more content about how they've struggled. Listening for examples of "clean" pain—such as loss, fear, or disappointment, which may be followed by efforts to move away—versus secondary emotions such as anger, frustration, or apathy might help guide you toward content the client is avoiding. These moments in therapy offer an opportunity for both you and the client to practice the skills of acceptance and willingness.

Acceptance and Willingness for the Therapist

Whether unintentional or by design, we therapists often have our own therapeutic goals for clients that can be about changing, reducing, or managing symptoms or problem behaviors. As in the approach with clients, the first step is to become aware of this agenda so the responses and messages you present in therapy won't inadvertently be more of the same (e.g., supporting the need to control or change thoughts, feelings, or experiences). The change agenda can also be built into the therapeutic context when clients are referred by primary care or other providers, for example, when the provider is concerned that the client isn't taking care of her health or wants her to "get therapy for depression." In these circumstances, you can acknowledge the explicit control agenda of the health care system and even use it to exemplify the universality of this agenda and areas where problem solving may or may not work. It's perfectly reasonable for you to use these therapeutic circumstances, as well as your own struggles with control in the therapeutic context, to bring clients in contact with the potential costs of experiential avoidance and to introduce acceptance and willingness as alternatives that may allow for choices and actions that are more workable and values consistent.

Strategies to Support Acceptance and Willingness

The metaphors and exercises that are primarily relevant to building psychological flexibility through acceptance and willingness generally fall into two categories. The first set of strategies is designed to bring the client into experiential contact with the unworkability of the control agenda and experiential avoidance. The second set of strategies focuses on introducing acceptance and willingness as alternatives to control and provides opportunities to experience and practice these skills. The sections below offer metaphors and exercises addressing both sets of strategies.

Metaphors and Exercises for Control as the Problem

You can begin the process of identifying control or experiential avoidance as the problem by asking questions about what brings the client to therapy. This will give you a picture of the unwanted thoughts, feelings, and experiences he is struggling with.

The next critical step is taking a nonjudgmental and exploratory stance and examining all of the different ways he's tried to fix the presenting problem. The client may not be intentionally engaging in these strategies or may be unaware of their purpose as avoidance tools. In any case, your task is to bring to light both internal control strategies (e.g., thought suppression, distraction) and external control strategies (e.g., substance use, isolation) and examine the benefits and costs of these strategies in both the short term and the long run. This may open the door to exploring the client's intentions behind a choice and determining if that choice resulted in his desired outcome. Examining the workability of the client's behavior, especially as it relates to how efforts to avoid unwanted thoughts and feelings may be limiting his life, can validate a sense of futility around the struggle to control private events, creating a space for other behavioral possibilities, such as acceptance and willingness. In ACT, this is referred to as creative hopelessness (Hayes et al., 1999, p. 90). In this section we present several metaphors and exercises that can enhance the client's contact with the unworkability and costs of experiential control and help develop the creative hopelessness stance.

◆ ◆ ◆

DON'T THINK ABOUT A PUPPY
(Niloofar Afari, 2012)

As with other exercises that involve trying not to think about something, whether chocolate cake (Hayes et al., 1999, pp. 124–125), a yellow jeep (Hayes, 2005, pp. 24–25), vanilla ice cream (Walser & Westrup, 2007, pp. 69–70), or a jelly donut (Zettle, 2007, p. 169), the objective of the exercise Don't Think About a Puppy is to demonstrate the paradox of thought suppression. Many clients struggle with trying to suppress unwanted thoughts or memories. However, in order to know not to think about the thought or memory, one has to first think about it. This exercise and others like it are an easy and nonthreatening way for clients to experience the futility of controlling thoughts.

> If you're willing, I'd like you to do a short exercise with me. For the next few seconds, I'd like you to not think about a puppy. You can think about anything else other than a puppy. If thoughts of a cute little puppy that wags his tail and jumps on you to lick your face come up, go ahead and push those thoughts away and don't think about them. You can think about anything else, but whatever you do, don't think about a puppy.

Some clients may respond to this exercise and other thought suppression exercises by attempting to replace one thought with another (e.g., thinking of a kitten rather than a puppy), which can give them the impression that they successfully avoided thinking of the original thought. In such situations, it's important to process all of the client's attempts to get rid of or suppress the unwanted thought by exploring the amount of effort required and her purpose in what she was doing (e.g., thinking of a kitten in order not to think of a puppy), since substituting one thought for another necessarily entails the unwanted thought. In addition, explore the frequency, duration, and intensity of thoughts about a puppy. Typically, clients notice that they didn't have any thoughts about puppies all day long—until they tried to not think about them, at which point those thoughts paradoxically increased. Even if a client "successfully" suppresses puppies with kittens, the puppies reappear, often with greater intensity, as soon as she lets go of the effort required to think about kittens.

◆　◆　◆

THE PENDULUM
(Mikael Odhage, 2011)

The Pendulum focuses on emotional control by using the back-and-forth movement of a pendulum as a metaphor for the paradoxical effects of attempting to control emotions. It also touches on willingness as an alternative to experiential control. While it's possible to use this script as a guided-imagery exercise (after situating the client in the room with a few deep breaths), it can be useful to conduct it using a desktop pendulum as a prop or swinging any weighted object. Conducting it as an interactive exercise enhances the experiential nature of this metaphor.

Imagine a feeling—any feeling or emotion. How long will it last? Now imagine a pendulum swinging freely. The higher you lift it in one direction, the more power you give it to swing up on the other side. Perhaps you'll notice the power of its swing in the weight and resistance of the bob—the weight at the bottom of the pendulum—as you let go.

Feelings are like the pendulum; they swing. That's unavoidable. You may like one side more than the other. Yet if you try to fight the swinging nature of the pendulum and get the bob high up on the side you prefer, you'll give it more power to rise high on the opposite side—the side you dislike. (If using a prop, you can encourage the client to lift the bob high on one side and let it go.) *You may be able to stop it for a short moment or lift it higher than its natural cycle. But doing so will take a lot of energy on your part, and it doesn't work anyway, since sooner or later the bob will end up on the side you dislike—along with all the extra power you've been giving it. That's just the way pendulums work: the higher you move the bob in one direction, the more powerful the movement in the opposite direction is. The pendulum may swing more for some people than for others. Some may like it, and others may get motion sickness from the movement.*

Now suppose there's another option here besides grabbing the bob and trying to move it in one direction or another. What if instead you could climb up the string to the attachment? Being up there means that you're willing to let the pendulum swing— you don't expend your energy on the pendulum, and you don't give the side you dislike any extra energy. At the attachment of the pendulum, you can let it swing without getting motion sickness. The whole of you isn't swayed by the swinging of the bob, but the swinging is still there.

Willingness is about how open you are to experiencing the natural swing of your emotions, thoughts, bodily sensations, and memories when they show up on one side, maybe in the form of happiness or fond memories, or on the other, as in sadness, disappointment, or anxiety. (In the preceding sentence, choose internal experiences relevant to the client.) *Your experience with the pendulum can tell you that when you aren't willing to have one side, you've got it. It's when you're really unwilling to have anxiety* (or another emotion relevant to the client's situation) *that anxiety is something to be really worried about. That's when you give anxiety more power by lifting the bob as high as you can to get rid of it.*

You've tried for so long to control the feelings and thoughts you dislike, and you've gotten more of the same. Now there's a choice here. Instead of trying to control the swing, you're free to climb to willingness—to the attachment point of the pendulum. From the attachment, you can willingly let the pendulum swing both ways. Sometimes there's anxiety, sometimes not. And in both cases, you won't end up in an unworkable struggle that will only lead to undesired consequences.

You can't control the swing. All you can control is whether you're grabbing the bob or sitting on the willingness attachment. Let me ask you now: are you open to exploring how life might be different if you shift your focus from riding on the bob to sitting on the willingness attachment?

◆   ◆   ◆

BALL IN A POOL

(Matthew Jepsen, 2012)

The metaphor Ball in a Pool can be used to convey the counterproductiveness of trying to control thoughts and feelings while also suggesting acceptance and willingness as alternatives.

What if what you're doing with these thoughts, memories, and feelings is like fighting with a ball in a pool? You don't like these things. You don't want them, and you want them out of your life. So you try to push the ball under the water and out of your consciousness. However, the ball keeps popping back up to the surface, so you have to keep pushing it down or holding it under the water. Struggling with the ball in this way keeps it close to you, and it's tiring and futile. If you were to let go of the ball, it would pop up and float on the surface near you, and you probably wouldn't like it. But if you let it float there for a while without grabbing it, it could eventually drift away to the other side of the pool. And even if it didn't, at least you'd be able to use your arms and enjoy your swim, rather than spending your time fighting.

◆   ◆   ◆

ROOM FULL OF DUCT TAPE

(Philippe Vuille, 2013)

The metaphor Room Full of Duct Tape highlights the costs of experiential avoidance and attempts at control in much the same way as the Hungry Tiger metaphor (Hayes, 2005, pp. 36–37). In this metaphor, the noise represents troubling thoughts and feelings, and the duct tape represents experiential avoidance and efforts at control. Over time, these strategies severely restrict existence.

Picture your life as a room. One day you notice that a pipe near the ceiling in a corner is dripping. The sound of the falling drops makes you nervous, and you'd like to get rid of it. So you repair the leak with a length of duct tape and your peace of mind is back—until the water finds its way through the tape and the dripping sound is back: plop…plop…plop… So you put another length of tape around the first repair and it's quiet again.

Of course the peace and quiet doesn't last very long. You have to fix the leak again and again. That's not a big problem since duct tape is pretty cheap and you always manage to keep a spare roll handy. This goes on for months or even years until one day you notice that these big clumsy repairs are slowly filling the room, leaving less and less space for you to live in and bringing the dripping nearer and nearer to you.

◆　◆　◆

BUILDING A HOUSE
(Nuno Ferreira, 2013)

The main objective of the Building a House metaphor is to highlight the costs of experiential avoidance and unworkable attempts at control. In addition, the metaphor also introduces the possibility of choosing alternative behaviors. While this metaphor was initially designed to be used with clients who are struggling with irritable bowel syndrome or other physical conditions and find themselves living a limited life, it can be used broadly to emphasize the unworkability of avoidance. Throughout the metaphor, you can solicit examples from the client's life in which she made similar trade-offs, for example, not attending a child's school event because of fear of physical pain, and therefore losing out on the opportunity to be an involved parent; or not going out on a date with her partner because she fears being embarrassed by the physical symptoms of her disorder, and therefore losing out on the intimacy of spending time with her partner.

Have you noticed that every time you avoid a situation or event because it might cause discomfort, you're also narrowing the options available to you? By avoiding the situation you may gain the benefit of perhaps feeling a bit more comfortable at the time. But you also aren't getting any of the benefits that could have resulted from stepping into that situation. It's a trade-off, right?

This is a good point at which to solicit examples from the client's life and ask if the trade-off was a good deal.

By avoiding situations because they might be uncomfortable, you're narrowing your life more and more. Living is very similar to building a house. To build a house you need construction materials, say bricks, and you have plenty of these lying around you—your experiences. In your life you've noticed that some of these bricks look nicer than others. Some of them are clean new bricks that represent pleasant

ACCEPTANCE AND WILLINGNESS

sensations, thoughts, memories, and feelings. Other bricks are broken or dirty or just don't look sturdy enough. These represent all of the difficult experiences you've been struggling with, such as symptoms and negative thoughts and feelings.

What would happen if you chose to build your house with only the nice new bricks? It would probably be a very small house, wouldn't it?

And what if the nice bricks were close to the nasty bricks or even underneath a pile of them? Isn't it the case that you've been so busy trying not to touch the nasty bricks that you've missed those nice hidden bricks? Wouldn't that narrow your living space even more?

You might say that you're glad to be living in a small house. However, every time you step out of the house, the nasty bricks will still be there waiting for you, getting in your way so you can't get more nice new bricks. You might eventually even reach the point where you don't leave the house anymore. That sounds like a big trade-off, doesn't it?

What would happen if you chose to build your house with all of the bricks you have at your disposal? What if what we can do here is about building a house with all of the bricks available so you can have a bit more room to live in? What if this is a space where you can learn how to live with both nice and nasty bricks in your house in the service of having a bigger life—one in which you'll have the choice to keep expanding? How does that sound?

◆　　◆　　◆

LIFE'S A BEACH: STRUGGLING IN THE RIP
(Ken Davis, 2013)

Although the metaphor Life's a Beach touches on all six of the ACT core concepts, it's primarily designed to capture the essence of creative hopelessness in a graphic manner. Because of its scope, it can be useful to present this metaphor early on in therapy and then refer back to it and highlight its various components as other ACT processes are addressed. It also can be especially helpful with clients who are experiencing anxiety or have obsessive thoughts and compulsive behaviors.

Sometimes life is like swimming at the beach. We launch headlong into life expecting to have a fun, relaxing, and refreshing time. People ply us with good advice: "Don't forget the sunscreen." "Swim between the flags." "Stay out of the water for thirty minutes after eating." "Watch out for sharks." So we jump in, splash around, and have a good time. Depending on your personality and experience, you may be carefree, or you might be anxiously watching for sharks or continually monitoring the flags to make sure you're in the right place. Or maybe you're the sort of person who loves to flout the rules, so you swim anywhere.

Suddenly your pleasure is interrupted by an unpleasant sensation. You're knocked off your feet. You can no longer touch the sandy bottom, and you notice that you're headed out to sea. You panic and immediately set the goal of getting back to shore and take action to achieve that goal. You do it without thinking. It's instinctive. You start paddling furiously against the rip current. Sometimes you seem to be making a little progress, but then you start to tire and notice that you're losing the battle. You swim harder. You roll over on your back and kick with your legs. But you're getting nowhere—and getting exhausted. You forget why you came to the beach in the first place. You begin to tell yourself, "If only I had stayed between the flags" or "I wish I'd done more swimming training before I risked it all by coming to the beach," but none of this wondering how you got into this position is any help. You're still paddling furiously and getting nowhere.

Maybe you call for help, and here I am, a lifesaver come to the rescue. So notice: Here I am with a board to rescue you, and I suggest that you grab the board. Before you can grab the board, you need to stop paddling furiously. Even though every fiber in your body screams in protest, you must stop paddling and try something different—grabbing the board.

Now, I'm a very contrary lifesaver. My job is not to rescue you, but to teach you to rescue yourself. The thing about life is that you can get sucked into a rip current at any time. That rip may be depression, grief, anxiety, or urges to eat, gamble, spend, or use drugs.

I want you to learn how to get out of trouble when you get stuck in a rip. So I invite you to swim slowly across the rip. I offer to swim alongside you. As you do this, you'll feel the tug of the rip. You'll get carried out to sea further than you'd like to be, and your mind will flash all sorts of scary scenarios before your eyes. That's what minds do. Mine does it too. I'm not asking you not to be scared, anxious, or depressed. I'm asking you to swim across the rip while experiencing those thoughts and sensations. Eventually you'll come to calm water and be able to get on with enjoying your day at the beach.

What I'm inviting you to do is to give up paddling furiously and allow the uncomfortable sensations and scary thoughts of being carried out to sea to be present. I'm inviting you to reconnect with what really matters: having fun at the beach for whatever reasons that's enjoyable for you. I'm inviting you to take effective action, and what that is depends on the situation. If you're safe, it means enjoying the sun and the surf for your own reasons. If you're stuck in a rip of (insert the presenting problem), it means stopping the struggle and taking small strokes in the direction of where you want to be, whatever experiences come up.

The following addition can highlight the problems with strict rule following and facilitate an exploration of the unworkability of buying into thoughts. Encourage clients to use their own examples of rules and advice they've been given and to examine their workability.

Do you remember all the good advice people have given you about how to be safe when going to the beach? Notice that some of it is good advice, like "Don't get out of your depth if you can't swim." Some is mostly right but sometimes wrong, like "It's safe to swim between the flags." And some is just urban myth, like "Rubbing butter on your skin protects you from sunburn." I'll bet you didn't ask for any of that advice; it just randomly came your way. People with good and maybe bad intentions filled your head with a mixture of good, bad, and neutral advice. So how do you tell whether any given bit of advice that pops into your head when you make plans to go to the beach is worth following?

The metaphor can also be expanded to generate a discussion of values and goals, including pursuing the same goal for different reasons and being able to move in valued directions even if a specific goal is blocked.

Notice that there are lots of people at the beach on a hot day. You can imagine that they aren't all there for the same reason. What are some of the reasons for going to the beach? Some people go to have fun with friends. Some go to relax and read. Some go to get a tan. Some go to cool down.

Encourage the client to generate responses for as wide a range of options as possible.

For example, you may be going to the beach (goal) to cool down (value). What if the road to the beach is closed? There are other ways to cool down. For example, you can sit in an air-conditioned room, take a cold shower, or drink an iced coffee.

You can add the following script to further address excessive problems with anxiety, worry, or obsessive-compulsive behaviors. This section may be particularly helpful for trauma survivors who have developed excessive or unrealistic safety concerns.

Notice that in this scenario there are precautions you can take to improve your safety. You can learn skills like how to do a survival stroke, or you can simply train to be a better swimmer. You can put on sunblock to prevent getting a sunburn. You can stay out of the surf on really rough days. You can avoid beaches where there are stinging jellyfish. You can swim between the flags. These can serve to improve your enjoyment of being at the beach. But what happens to your fun if you become obsessed with safety? What if instead of floating around or catching waves, you keep your eyes glued on the flags? Or what if as soon as your toes hit the water you run back to your bag to put on more sunblock? What if you give up on going to the beach because it's too dangerous?

Here, allow the client to answer, then discuss reasonable safety and how to practice it, as well as willingness to have worry thoughts while pursuing a valued activity.

Notice also that despite your best efforts, you can still get stuck in a rip. Winds, current, and tide may change, and an area that had been safe turns into a rip. Or maybe a huge sneaker wave comes and knocks you off your feet and into a rip. It doesn't matter whose fault it was or how it happened. Once you're in a rip you have an important choice to make: Keep struggling and eventually succumb to exhaustion and drown, or stop struggling and start taking effective action by swimming across the rip toward your values.

◆ ◆ ◆

THE CIRCUS ACT: JUGGLING AND HULA HOOPS
(Jill Stoddard, 2013)

The Circus Act is another metaphor that illustrates the futility of control. However, its main focus is to show that some control often seems possible at first (i.e., clients think they're doing it well), but over time it ends up greatly restricting life. If you have several hula hoops or juggling balls, using these props will enhance the impact of this metaphor. If you don't have actual props, you can demonstrate with hand gestures for a more experiential quality.

Trying to control your thoughts and feelings is like being part of a circus act—one with jugglers in one ring and hula hoopers in another. Just about anyone can toss one ball back and forth. Lots of people can even juggle two balls. Likewise, it's pretty easy to get a single hula hoop to circle your hips a few times. Similarly, it might seem like suppressing your thoughts or avoiding feelings is doable and effective and doesn't come at much of a cost. But what happens as you add more balls or hula hoops? You have to concentrate more to keep things going. In fact, you can hardly concentrate on anything else. After a while, all of those balls and hula hoops restrict your movement. And pretty soon, the balls and hoops all come crashing down on you. Something that started out as simple and harmless becomes impossible to keep up.

Metaphors and Exercises for Acceptance and Willingness

Once clients have experienced the unworkability of the control agenda, the focus of therapy shifts to introducing acceptance and willingness as alternatives, providing opportunities to experience and practice these skills in session, and bringing willingness to different areas of life. As seen in the scripts above, the initial metaphors and exercises used to address the futility and costs of experiential avoidance hint at acceptance and willingness as alternatives. However, at this point clients are often confused about what these alternatives mean. They may struggle with letting go of comparisons to their past or an imagined future life or mistake willingness for the *desire* to have a feeling, thought, or experience. They may also focus on understanding acceptance and willingness intellectually, often as an end point, like a feeling—which again can lead to inflexible action—instead of an ongoing process or stance.

Your task is to teach what acceptance and willingness are, not only by describing them as active processes of nonjudgmental openness to and awareness of all of one's experiences, but also by demonstrating acceptance and willingness and creating opportunities for clients to experience these stances. This can occur throughout the course of therapy and take many forms. For example, giving the client the choice of whether to participate in an exercise by first asking, "Are you willing to…?" is a very simple way of giving him an opportunity to practice the willingness stance. Other in-session examples include catching a client moving away from emotional content and bringing him back to gently sit with the feelings and note their characteristics (e.g., associated thoughts, bodily sensations, and urges) or directly eliciting difficult material that the two of you can then process together.

You also can demonstrate the act of willingness by noting your own difficult thoughts, feelings, and reactions to material in the session—for example, by saying, "As we're sitting here and talking, I'm feeling a growing sense of frustration, and this thought is showing up that I have to do something different or teach you better or help you get what we're talking about. I'm having this urge to jump in and fix things. And, I'm going to sit here, be present to you, and share in your frustration and sadness." Aside from taking advantage of opportunities to practice acceptance and willingness in session, you can work with the client to identify opportunities for acts of acceptance and willingness outside of therapy, both large and small, through what would traditionally be called exposure, as a way to practice willingly experiencing and feeling whatever shows up.

Metaphors and exercises targeting acceptance and willingness are used throughout the course of treatment, first to introduce these concepts, and then to encourage contact with increasingly difficult private events in the service of values-driven action. The approaches below cover a broad range of acceptance and willingness exercises and metaphors.

♦ ♦ ♦

YES AND NO
(Robyn Walser & Niloofar Afari, 2012)

The Yes and No exercise is an adaptation of an exercise presented by Tara Brach in her groundbreaking book *Radical Acceptance* (Brach, 2003). While Brach's approach focuses on saying yes to emotions that may arise in difficult situations, such as anger, fear, or sadness, this adaptation uses a yes or no strategy to bring clients into experiential contact with how it feels to resist versus accept an experience, even one potentially as neutral as sitting in a chair.

> *In this exercise, I'm going to ask you to avoid experiencing the sensations you have of your back against the chair you're sitting in. For the next two to three minutes, whenever you notice a sensation of your back against the chair, I want you to say no to those sensations.*

You can expand on this exercise by having the client first say no to the physical sensations of her back against the chair, and then say no to any thoughts and emotions that show up about the sensations or even the exercise more generally.

Be sure to allow a full two to three minutes for the experience of saying no. While this can seem like a long time, it's important to allow sufficient time for the client to come in contact with multiple sensations of her back against the chair and the experience of avoiding those sensations. Remind the client from time to time to continue to say no to the sensations.

Once you've allowed enough time, refocus the client's attention to the room. Ask her what sensations came up and what it was like to say no to these sensations. Help her distinguish between the physical sensations and the thoughts and feelings that accompanied resistance.

> *Okay, now I'd like to do the same exercise, except now rather than avoiding the sensations of your back against the chair, I'd like you to be willing to feel the those sensations, simply as sensations, whatever they may be, positive or negative: pain, discomfort, tingling, warmth, coolness, and so on. Whatever those sensations are, I'd like you to say yes to them.*

Again, be sure to wait the full two to three minutes, offering occasional reminders to continue saying yes, before refocusing the client's attention to the room. Ask her to describe the physical sensations and the thoughts and feelings that came up. Help her reflect on the difference in her experiences with saying yes and no as it may relate to willingness and control strategies.

◆　◆　◆

HOLDING A PEN
(Pia Heppner, 2013)

The exercise Holding a Pen may be appropriate for situations in which a client is engaging in a significant amount of effort, mental as well as behavioral, to resolve an external problem, but the nature of the problem is such that the outcome isn't directly under his control. This might be a complex situation in which both effort and a stance of holding his experience lightly are required in pursuit of a goal. He may be engaging in more worry or planning, perhaps while continuing to do what's needed to some degree, and may be getting increasingly frustrated that his desired outcome remains elusive. This exercise is useful with agendas that are goal-directed and external, such as finding employment or securing housing, when the intensity of effort results in increased frustration, anger, and exhaustion, but the client remains inflexible and doesn't recognize that he has a choice to de-escalate his efforts while still remaining goal directed.

The transcript below demonstrates willingness to continue engaging in helpful action while holding this action lightly. The client is unemployed and has spent the last six months applying for jobs, attending job fairs, and searching for work on the Internet for hours on end, but he has only been invited for a handful of interviews and hasn't received any formal job offers. He has become increasingly irritable and despondent.

Therapist:　You seem rather quiet today. What's been going on for you?

Client: I can't seem to get any breaks. I feel like I've been hitting the pavement as hard as I can, looking for work, anything. And still... nothing. I just get e-mails telling me, "Thanks for applying, but we've hired someone else for the position." I'm just getting tired of it.

Therapist: That sounds pretty frustrating. Tell me about your job search. What sorts of things are you doing to look for work?

Client: I basically wake up and start my day on the computer and spend anywhere from two to four hours straight just going through websites—anything I can find that lists job postings. I've even got four different versions of my résumé ready, just to be sure I can be considered for different positions.

Therapist: It sounds like you really are "hitting the pavement." How much time are you spending during the day focused on your job search?

Client: It seems like day and night. It's all I think about, even when I'm trying not to think about it. When I'm watching TV or going for a walk, it's right there.

Therapist: What happens for you when you start thinking about it?

Client: I get this panicky feeling and my chest gets tight...like I can't handle it.

Therapist: How about at night? Do you find yourself thinking about it then too?

Client: Night is the worst. I lie there and worry about losing my apartment and how little money I have left. I feel like all I can do is just keep looking for work or try to shut all of this out.

Therapist: It seems like you're really giving this 100 percent...

Client: More like 150 percent.

Therapist: Yes, and in spite of your best efforts, you still haven't received a job offer, like you've been hoping.

Client: Getting those e-mails is the worst. I feel like such a failure.

Therapist: I can see that it's really getting you down. (*Pauses.*) I'm wondering if you're willing to try something with me. (*Offers the client a pen.*) Are you willing to take this pen and hold it in your hand?

Client: (*Grasps the pen.*) All right.

Therapist: Now see if you can hold this pen as hard as you've been working on trying to find a job. Think of all the time, effort, and desire you've put into looking for work and grip that pen as hard as the effort you've been putting in. Do you feel that?

Client: (*Grasps the pen visibly harder.*) Yeah.

Therapist: How tightly are you holding it on a scale of 1 to 10, 10 being the tightest?

Client: A 10 for sure. You wouldn't be able to pry it out of my hands.

Therapist: Okay, now I want you to see if you can hold on to the pen, but maybe see if you can bring that 10 down to a 5. Do you feel that?

Client: (*Pauses.*) Yeah. I think it's like a 5.

Therapist: Now see if you can bring it down even more. See if you can bring it down to only as much of a grip as you need to keep the pen in your hand without dropping it. Do you feel that?

Client: Hmm, okay. (*The therapist gives the client time.*) I'm there.

Therapist: Notice what that feels like, to hold the pen lightly and just enough. Notice how even though it's not a 10, you're still holding the pen and it hasn't dropped to the floor. (*Pauses.*) Do you think you can continue to do the things you need to do to look for work but not have to do them at the level of a 10?

Client: (*Pauses.*) So maybe not go into each thing with such full force?

Therapist: Yes, still doing those things, keeping your feet moving, but maybe on the back end not gripping so tightly to what you want to happen.

Client: (*Pauses.*) I guess I can do that.

It's worthwhile to use the experience of holding the pen lightly to generate a discussion of what holding the job search lightly will look like and what the client might do differently. Of course, this exercise can be adapted to fit other client content.

◆ ◆ ◆

COMPASSION

(Robyn Walser, 2012)

For many clients, acceptance can take the form of having compassion for others and self, by holding suffering and emotional pain kindly. Self-compassion may be particularly difficult for veterans, who may evaluate themselves as unworthy or broken in the context of their wartime experiences and behavior (e.g., not being able to save a buddy or having to shoot into a house full of children). While they may be willing to express compassion for others, they find it difficult to receive compassion from others and even more challenging to extend compassion to themselves.

This exercise, based on the writing of the Dalai Lama and some of the work at Stanford University's Center for Compassion and Altruism Research and Education (Jinpa, 2010), was designed by Robyn Walser for the therapist manual *Acceptance and Commitment Therapy for Depression in Veterans* (Walser, Sears, Chartier, & Karlin, in press). Its purpose is to help clients experientially get in touch with compassionate feelings for others, and then practice turning it toward themselves. It's preferable to conduct this exercise as an eyes-closed exercise so clients can maintain their focus on the thoughts and feelings that arise. For clients who have difficulty with closing their eyes, ask them to maintain their visual focus on a point on the horizon or a fixed point on the floor.

This exercise is about compassion, the feeling of empathy we can have when someone is suffering or in emotional pain. As a way to get more in touch with feelings of compassion, I'd like to ask you to do an exercise with me in which you focus on compassionate feelings you've experienced. I'm going to ask you to close your eyes and follow my guidance. Throughout, I'll ask some questions that you can answer with your eyes closed.

Now, if you're willing, go ahead and get settled into your chair. Take a few deep breaths, in and out, and close your eyes. See if you can think back to an experience you've had where you felt compassion for someone, witnessed compassion by others, or imagined that it would have been helpful to have compassion. It might have been a time when you were younger or a more recent time. I'd like you to get that previous experience or specific situation in mind, when you felt or saw or imagined compassion toward someone. You can probably see the details of that situation in your mind's eye: what was happening, how you were feeling, how you expressed yourself, and so on. Go ahead and focus on this experience for the next few minutes. You can use your breath to anchor yourself throughout the exercise.

After pausing for up to five minutes, reconnect with the client by gently letting him know that you'll be asking some questions. Be sure to allow enough time for him to respond to each question and discuss as necessary.

That's right...breathing in and out while you focus on the experience of compassion toward someone. Now I'd like to ask you a few questions while you continue to breathe with your eyes closed. What was your experience during this exercise?... Were you able to get in touch with the experience of compassion?... What did it feel like?... How difficult was it?... How did the experience change over time?...

Now that you've connected with what it felt like to show or see compassion toward someone else, I'd like to move on to when others have shown compassion toward you. I'd like you to think about a time or specific situation in which you were challenged by something or were in pain and one or more people showed you compassion. See if you can get that specific situation in mind and focus on it for a few minutes. Again, you can use your breath to anchor yourself throughout the exercise.

After pausing for up to five minutes, reconnect with the client by gently letting him know that you'll be asking some questions again. As before, be sure to allow enough time for him to respond to each question and discuss as necessary.

What was your experience during this exercise?... Were you able to get in touch with the experience of compassion?... What did it feel like?... How difficult was it?... How did the experience change over time?... What were your reactions to receiving compassion?... What kinds of thoughts, feelings, and sensations did it produce?...

Now that you've cultivated a sense of compassion for someone else and experienced what it feels like to receive compassion from others, I'm going to ask you to take the same sense of compassion and turn it toward yourself. See if you can imagine yourself in a similar situation of pain or a time of needing compassion from others. Alternatively, you can focus on the present moment—right now—and, for a few moments, practice this experience of giving yourself the compassion you might normally save for others. Take a few minutes to get in touch with what you need and what giving yourself compassion looks like. Notice your reactions to doing this: the kinds of thoughts, feelings, and sensations it produces for you.

It's best to allow enough time for the client to process this exercise, and for the two of you to discuss the client's experiences and potential barriers as he moved from compassion toward others to self-compassion. In addition, the two of you can identify small acts of self-compassion that the client can practice between sessions.

◆　◆　◆

CHILD

(Walser & Westrup, 2007, pp. 186–188)

The Child guided imagery exercise was developed by Robyn Walser and Darrah Westrup based on the Observer exercise outlined in the seminal ACT text by Hayes and colleagues (1999, pp. 192–196). This exercise can be quite powerful and is often used toward the end of treatment when clients have had ample opportunities to practice acceptance and willingness in various life domains. Clients typically don't have much difficulty with this exercise, but some do get caught up in the content of visiting their childhood home and may lose contact with the meaning of the exercise. Thus, it's important for you to fully understand the function of this exercise—to give oneself compassion and self-acceptance—and take an active role in guiding the imagery of the exercise. Of note, what the client asks of each parent and the adult self in the exercise is not a physical or material object but rather a value, like love, support, or protection, or an action that signifies these values.

> *If you're willing, I'd like us to do an eyes-closed exercise that focuses on acceptance. This is going to last a little longer than some of the other exercises we've done, so you'll want to sit in a position where you're comfortable but alert.* (Pause to allow adequate time for this to occur.)
>
> *I'd like you to close your eyes and take just a moment to focus on your breathing, as we've done many times in the past.* (Allow the client to focus on breathing for about a minute.) *Now I'd like you to search back through your memories to a time when you remember feeling a little sad or lonely, perhaps when you were six or seven, maybe a little older or a little younger. Picture what you looked like at that age. Imagine how small your hands were and the type of clothing you wore. Perhaps imagine yourself in one of your favorite outfits.*
>
> *Now put yourself in the place of this child, as if you have become that child and are looking through her eyes. Look down and see your small hands and the clothes you're wearing. Now imagine that you're going back to the place where you lived when you were that age. If you can't picture your exact home at that age, choose one that you can picture. Once you have the image, imagine that you're standing before the home as that child. Imagine walking up to the front door and reaching up to take the doorknob, turning it to open the door, and stepping through. Look around and notice the pictures on the walls, the furniture. ... Notice how you have to look up to see some things given how small you are.*

Now I'd like you to go to the place in your home where you might find your mother or mother figure…the place where she would hang out. When you've found her, notice what she's doing. Look around and see the room. Walk up to your mother and do whatever you have to do to get her attention, so that she looks you right in the face. Once she looks, from that place of one of your early hurts, ask her for what you need. … Tell her what you need and see if she can give it. (Pause to allow time for the client to complete the request.)

Now, gently pulling away from this interaction with your mother, I'd like you to go find your father or father figure. Go to the place in your home where he might hang out. When you find him, notice what he's doing. Look around the room and see what's there. Now walk up to your father and do whatever you have to do to get his attention and get him to look you right in the face. Once you have his attention, ask him for what you need in response to the early hurt you've chosen. Tell him what you need and see if he can give it. (Pause to allow time for the client to complete the request.)

Now gently leave your father and begin to walk to the front door. When you arrive, reach up, turn the knob, and open the door. Step through and pull the door closed behind you. Begin to walk away from the house, heading down the sidewalk or street. … And as you do this, notice that in the distance you see someone walking toward you, an adult. As you get closer, you realize that it's you. It's the adult you are today. Go up to the adult you see before you and do whatever you have to do to get her attention so that she looks you right in the face. Once you have her attention, from the place of hurt, ask her for what you need. (Pause to allow time for the client to complete the request.)

Now gently bring yourself back to the room, picture it, and return when you're ready.

While the exercise can end as indicated above, Walser and Westrup suggest the following addition to further the intended impact of the experience. You can add it just before asking the client to come back to the room.

Now imagine that you're leaving this scene of meeting the adult you on the sidewalk, and imagine that you're transported back to this very moment, to this room, this chair. You are now the adult that you know today. And now imagine that the little child, the child you were just a moment ago, is standing right outside the door of this room. She's opening the door and stepping inside. Imagine that she's walking toward you and comes up to stand right before you. As she stands there, give her your attention. … Look her right in the face and see what she needs. See if you can give it.

53

(Pause to allow time for the client to complete the request.) Notice if there's any withholding in you. Check to see whether you're resisting anything. If so, see if you can let that go and give the child what she needs. Now imagine that the child is climbing into your lap. … Imagine that she's melting into you, becoming a part of you. (Pause.)

Now gently bring yourself back to the room, picture it, and return when you're ready.

Clients who are struggling with depression or who have an extensive history of trauma have often bought into negative experiences and messages that give rise to guilt and shame, and have turned away from the self. While they may benefit greatly from this exercise, they are also likely to describe an inability to accept the young self and to give what's being asked of them. Your ability to process this exercise with the client, orient her toward self-acceptance as a choice, and work through the barriers to self-acceptance is critical.

◆ ◆ ◆

EATING AN APPLE

(Caitlin Ferriter, 2013)

The metaphor Eating an Apple is useful as an introduction to the concept of acceptance. It may also be useful in circumstances when a client is struggling against a life change (e.g., children leaving home, diagnosis of a chronic illness, or retirement) when there's a substantial pull for the client to compare how things were in the past to how things are now.

Acceptance is like eating an apple. One reason for eating an apple could be because you're trying to lose weight, so you're trying to stay away from things that are "bad" for you. So instead of your usual snack of a cupcake, you tell yourself you'll have an apple. You may "choose" an apple, but what will it be like to eat that apple? As you eat it, you start comparing it to the cupcake. With each bite, you're thinking about how the apple isn't as sweet, fudgy, and good as the cupcake. Then, when you're done, you eat the cupcake anyway. What we're talking about here is another way to eat an apple: allowing the apple to be an apple, rather than needing or wanting it to be something it's not…noticing the crispiness of each bite, the juiciness, and the sweetness for what it is and not for what it isn't—a cupcake.

◆ ◆ ◆

CRYING BABY ON THE PLANE
(Caitlin Ferriter, 2013)

Clients occasionally confuse acceptance and willingness with the desire to experience something. Upon an initial discussion of willingness, they often say they don't want whatever it is that brings them to therapy. Using a situation that most people are likely to have experienced firsthand, the Crying Baby on the Plane metaphor can highlight the distinction between being willing to have an experience and wanting or desiring that experience.

Imagine yourself sitting on a plane for an overnight flight. You have the whole row to yourself and think, Perfect! I can stretch out and really get some sleep. *Then, just before the cabin door is closed, a young couple comes on board with a screaming baby. You think to yourself, "The poor people who have to sit next to them all night!" Just as that thought crosses your mind, you see the couple moving toward you. They're seated next to you! You shuffle your stuff to make room for them, but in your head you're saying,* Noooooo! *They smile and thank you for helping them get to their seats, and all the while their baby is screaming.*

They try everything to soothe him. They try the bottle, and that just makes him scream louder. They try his favorite toy, but he keeps screaming. What are your options here? You can spend the next eight hours giving them dirty looks, scoffing at their failed attempts to quiet their child, and letting them know that this kind of behavior is absolutely unacceptable on a plane. Alternatively, you could join them in trying to quiet the child: playing peekaboo, giving the child your phone to fiddle with—doing anything to shut the kid up. Or, you could choose to do what you would otherwise do on an overnight flight while taking in the sounds of that child as they are and recognizing that the child is doing exactly what children do—not wanting or liking the sounds the child is making, but also not needing the sounds not to be there. And all the while, you're also noticing that no matter how long the child cries, he won't cry forever, and that wanting him to quiet down will never be what's needed to quiet him.

◆ ◆ ◆

UNDERSTANDING THE CAR
(Hank Robb, 2012)

Intellectual understanding is important to some clients, and they may use it as an experiential avoidance strategy that poses a barrier to acceptance. The metaphor Understanding the Car uses a client's own experience to suggest that understanding isn't necessarily a prerequisite to acceptance and willingness. This may be especially useful when the client is invested in understanding why he feels or thinks a certain way. The metaphor assumes some familiarity with cars. If that isn't the case for a particular client, you can adapt the metaphor to fit the client's experiences, for example, substituting a computer or a cell phone for the car.

> *I'm sure you know that these days cars are like large, moving computers, with big and small computer chips that control everything from temperature to the brake system. Now, except for folks who work with computer chips or cars, very few people understand how computer chips work. Do you know all the intricate details of how computer chips work? (Clients invariably say they don't.)*
>
> *I understand that you came here in a car, and that car probably has one or more computer chips in it. So, let me ask you this: After our session, will you stand next to your car until you understand how it works, or will you accept that it works, get in it, and drive home? If your goal is to get home, how will understanding the car help you get there?*

Clients often chuckle and agree that they'll drive their car even if they don't understand how it works, and that furthering their understanding of the car won't help them get home. You can then relate this experience to their desire to understand feelings and thoughts when doing so won't help them move in valued directions and may even be a barrier (i.e., standing by the car instead of driving).

◆ ◆ ◆

ENGAGING THE CLUTCH
(Randall Wilson, 2013)

The metaphor Engaging the Clutch touches on the mind traps associated with the control agenda and highlights the interconnectedness of willingness, values, and committed action. For those who may not be familiar with a manual transmission, it might be useful to describe the function of a clutch (to disengage the engine from the transmission in order to change gears), but this isn't necessary.

It's as if you're driving a car on your journey through life. However, you begin to notice that the engine in this car is very finicky, almost like it has a mind of its own. It occasionally revs up very high or bogs down low. In the process, the car speeds up or slows to a crawl, regardless of the speed limit, upcoming turns, or what the traffic is like around you. Naturally, this makes it difficult for you to effectively drive in the direction you want to go. Your initial response is to try to control the pace of the engine by hitting the brakes when it speeds up and hitting the gas when it slows down. In response to the engine acting up, you slam on the brakes or press the gas pedal for all you're worth. However, over time you notice that this doesn't work very well or for very long. In fact, the engine revs up even higher or bogs down even lower when you try to fight it. What's more, when you're putting all of your energy into those pedals, your attention is no longer on the road or the direction you're headed.

What if there were an alternative to the gas pedal and the brakes? What if you looked down to find that there was a clutch pedal hidden in a dark corner of the floorboard? Instead of trying to control the finicky, unpredictable engine, you simply take the car out of gear. This eliminates the need to control or change the pace of the engine. Whenever it begins to race or bog down, you simply push in the clutch. Then, when the pace of the engine is appropriate or effective for the road that you're on, you let the clutch back out. The engine no longer controls the speed of the car. You do. Now you're free to concentrate on the road ahead of you.

We can think of our minds as being like the engine in this example, and willingness, acceptance, and mindful awareness as all being like the clutch. When the mind begins racing, telling us to run away or escape, showing us images of possible dangerous scenarios, reminding us of painful past events, or bogging us down with evaluations, judgments, and negative predictions, we can choose to engage the clutch and willingly observe these things without allowing our behavior—the car itself—to automatically speed up or slow down. When we find that the mind is being helpful, we can release the clutch and allow it to do its work. We can never successfully gain control of the engine, but we can gain control of the speed and direction of the car.

Summary

Acceptance and willingness, which are directly linked to values and committed action, are ongoing processes that are relevant throughout the course of treatment. In this chapter we reviewed the core concepts of acceptance and willingness as well as techniques you can use to address these concepts. We also selectively highlighted a number of metaphors and exercises that are intended to bring clients into experiential contact with the costs of control while introducing acceptance and willingness as alternatives. Other exercises offered here are designed to increase psychological flexibility. We've chosen to underscore self-compassion and self-acceptance because, in our experience, a pervasive sense of unworthiness is, for some people, the last stand against willingness and choosing to live in alignment with their values.

Metaphors and Exercises Targeting Acceptance, Willingness, and Control as the Problem

Metaphors and Exercises in This Chapter

- Don't Think About a Puppy

- The Pendulum

- Ball in a Pool

- Room Full of Duct Tape

- Building a House

- Life's a Beach: Struggling in the Rip

- The Circus Act: Juggling and Hula Hoops

- Yes and No

- Holding a Pen

- Compassion

- Child

- Eating an Apple

- Crying Baby on the Plane

- Understanding the Car

- Engaging the Clutch

In addition, the following exercises and metaphors, available in the sources cited, also target acceptance, willingness, and control as the problem.

Other Exercises

- Accepting Yourself on Faith (Hayes et al., 1999, pp. 263–264)

- Being Willingly Out of Breath (Hayes, 2005, pp. 49–51)

- Carrying Your Depression (Zettle, 2007, pp. 110–111)

- Chinese Finger Cuffs (Eifert & Forsyth, 2005, pp. 146–149)

- Chocolate Cake (Hayes et al., 1999, pp. 124–125)

- Compassion Mindfulness (Walser & Westrup, 2007, p. 141)

- Don't Think About Your Thoughts (Hayes, 2005, pp. 25–26)

- Empty Chair (Hayes et al., 1999, pp. 257–258)

- Feeling Good (Hayes et al., 1999, p. 145)

- Giving Your Target a Form (Hayes, 2005, pp. 138–140)

- Hands-On (Walser & Westrup, 2007, pp. 89–90)

- Jump (Hayes et al., 1999, pp. 240–241)

- Looking for Mr. Discomfort (Hayes et al., 1999, pp. 246–247)

- The Pain Is Gone, Now What? (Hayes, 2005, pp. 14–15)

- Recognizing Mind-Quality Mindfulness (Walser & Westrup, 2007, pp. 112–113)

- Rules of the Game (Hayes et al., 1999, pp. 145–146)

- A Screw, a Toothbrush, and a Lighter (Hayes, 2005, pp. 21–22)

- Sitting with Feelings (Zettle, 2007, pp. 112–113)

- Tin Can Monster (Hayes et al., 1999, pp. 171–174)

- Welcome Anxiety (Walser & Westrup, 2007, pp. 87–88)

- What Are the Numbers? (Hayes et al., 1999, pp. 126–128)

- A Yellow Jeep (Hayes, 2005, pp. 24–25)

- Your Suffering Inventory (Hayes, 2005, pp. 12–13)

Other Metaphors

- Box Full of Stuff (Hayes et al., 1999, pp. 136–138)
- Chinese Handcuffs (Hayes et al., 1999, pp. 104–105)
- Expanding Balloon (Hayes et al., 1999, p. 248)
- Falling in Love (Zettle, 2007, pp. 170–171)
- Feedback Screech (Hayes et al., 1999, p. 108)
- Fighting the Wave (Walser & Westrup, 2007, pp. 75–76)
- High School Sweetheart (Hayes et al., 1999, p. 252)
- The Hungry Tiger (Hayes, 2005, pp. 36–37)
- Joe the Bum (Hayes et al., 1999, pp. 239–240)
- Passengers on the Bus (Hayes et al., 1999, pp. 157–158)
- Polygraph (Hayes et al., 1999, pp. 123–124)
- Quicksand (Hayes, 2005, pp. 3–4)
- The Shark Tank Polygraph (Hayes, 2005, p. 30)
- Swamp (Hayes et al., 1999, pp. 247–248)
- Take Your Keys with You (Hayes et al., 1999, pp. 248–250)
- Tug-of-War with a Monster (Hayes et al., 1999, p. 109)
- Two Scales (Hayes et al., 1999, pp. 133–134)
- Worm on a Hook (Walser & Westrup, 2007, p. 173)

CHAPTER 4

COGNITIVE DEFUSION

In ACT, cognitive fusion refers to the human tendency to become entangled with thoughts as a result of a strong belief in their literal content. In other words, we listen to and believe what our minds tell us. Of course buying into thoughts isn't always problematic. When your mind tells you how to balance your checkbook or drive your car safely, listening may be adaptive. But what happens when your mind says you're boring or unattractive? Fusion with these kinds of thoughts will probably result in experiential avoidance. Specifically, you may avoid social or romantic interactions even if being close with others is very important to you. In this way, cognitive fusion pulls us away from living in alignment with our values.

Fusion is most likely to arise across six cognitive domains: rules, reasons, judgments, past, future, and self (Harris, 2009):

- **Rules.** Rule-governed thinking often consists of "should," "must," "ought" and "if-then" language. You may have a client who thinks, *If I'm in therapy, then it must mean I'm crazy. I should be more normal. If people know how messed up I really am, they will never accept me.* Fusion with rule-governed thinking equates to inflexibility, which invariably results in suffering.

- **Reasons.** Reason-governed thinking typically consists of excuses for why change is impossible. Clients may have thoughts such as *I don't have the willpower to change, I'm not smart enough (strong enough, capable enough, etc.), I'm too lazy (ill, unlucky, etc.),* or *My craving (anxiety, depression, etc.) is too strong to battle.* Fusion with reason-governed thinking holds clients back from making meaningful changes even when those changes are in line with important life values.

- **Judgments.** Fusion with judgments can pose a problem whether those evaluations are negative (e.g., *I'm so ugly* or *This anxiety is unbearable!*) or positive. For example, consider a client who puts friends, colleagues, family members, or helping professionals up on a pedestal and is chronically disappointed when they don't live up to her expectations.

- **Past and future.** Fusion with the past or future can involve both unpleasant and pleasant content: fusion with negative memories, wishing to recapture positive experiences from the past, getting hooked by fears about the future, or wishing for brighter days ahead. All of these forms of fusion pull clients out of their present moment. Sometimes this process serves as a cognitive form of experiential avoidance, and although this may produce mild, temporary relief, in the long term it only results in suffering. Ultimately, like all types of fusion, it tends to pull people away from the things that are most important to them. If, for example, a client is getting hooked by thoughts like *The last time I interviewed for a job, it was a total disaster; the next time is bound to be the same,* he's likely to avoid future job interviews, even if career development is a meaningful life pursuit for him.

- **Self.** Thoughts about the self are stories we tell that make up our sense of identity. They typically begin with "I am," and in ACT, they're referred to as the conceptualized self. This type of fusion leads people to be driven by the stories they have about themselves (e.g., *I am a tough-as-nails third-generation cop*), rather than by their values (e.g., *I want to be a loving, tender father to my daughter*). (We will discuss this form of fusion in greater detail in chapter 6, on self-as-context.)

The Function of Defusion in ACT

Insofar as cognitive fusion is the process by which we get hooked by the content of our thoughts, cognitive defusion is the process by which we change our relationship with our thoughts by stepping back and simply witnessing their presence. When we defuse, we disentangle from our self-talk and observe cognitions as entities separate from ourselves—as just words. This allows us to look *at* our thoughts rather than *from* them.

Consider this example: If you have the thought *Presenting at a professional conference is too scary; my colleagues will think I'm an incompetent fraud,* you can probably see that fusion with this thought is likely to result in avoidance of professional presentations. While this avoidance would certainly reduce anxiety in the short term, it would also mean missing out on an important professional opportunity, and the anxiety would persist in the long run. What if instead you simply witnessed what the mind says in much the same way you might watch a screen saver scroll across your computer or stock market symbols glide past on an electronic ticker tape? Imagine how your behavior might be different if you chose to see this thought as simply some words that may or may not be true. Ultimately, like acceptance and willingness, defusion creates wiggle room to make valued choices. In other words, if buying the thought *Presenting at a professional conference is too scary; my colleagues will think I'm an incompetent fraud* causes you to avoid professional presentations, simply observing the thought gives you the space to make a different choice. Importantly, this doesn't mean the thought disappears; it simply means you're making a choice to not be driven by its content. Thus, you are freed to continue moving in directions that are important to you—perhaps, for example, disseminating your expert knowledge to your colleagues.

As with all the core ACT concepts, and because cognitive fusion is a problem with literal language, ACT aims to achieve defusion experientially. Two broad categories of exercises have been created to facilitate the defusion process. The first involves stepping back and observing the content of the mind. This can be achieved through any number of symbolic representations. The computer screen saver and stock ticker tape mentioned above are just two examples. We encourage you to generate your own versions for specific clients. For example, if you're treating a pilot or aviation aficionado, you might use the image of a skywriting airplane or an airplane pulling a banner across the sky. The idea is to create a way for clients to take their thoughts and look *at* them—to see them out in front of themselves, as separate from the mind. The first set of exercises below (Defusion Exercises for Stepping Back and Observing), offers a number of great interventions that facilitate this process.

The second category of defusion exercises targets a deliteralization of language. The aim is to show language for what it is: a verbal production of sounds and syllables. When thoughts can be heard as noise or observed dispassionately, people can base choices to take action on the workability of the action rather than the believability or literality of thoughts or language. For example, a client might avoid taking professional or interpersonal risks because she's fused with the literal content of the thought *If I try, I will surely fail.* To facilitate defusion through deliteralization, you might have her sing this thought or say it in the voice of a cartoon character. The second set of exercises in this chapter (Defusion Exercises for Deliteralizing Language) offers scripts for some fun and creative approaches to facilitating this process. However, do note that because these exercises tend to be fun and even silly, some clients may experience them as invalidating. Therefore it's critical to conduct them in the context of genuine compassion for the pain clients endure.

In addition to the two types of experiential exercises described above, metaphors can also be used to illustrate defusion. We recommend experimenting with a combination of participatory exercises and illustrative metaphors to see what works best for particular clients.

As you go through the exercises and metaphors presented below, you'll find suggestions for how you might use some of them with specific populations. As with all of the exercises and metaphors in this book, you can use these scripts verbatim, or you can flexibly apply them however they best fit a particular client. After working with any metaphor or exercise, take a few minutes to discuss clients' experience with them. What did they notice? Where did they get caught up or stuck? How do they interpret the metaphor, and how does it connect with their experience? Have them continue to practice these exercises between sessions and ask them to notice how their experience does or doesn't change.

Be aware that many clients will experience defusion as watching thoughts "go away" and have the experience of "feeling better" when the words no longer hold the same emotional impact. As the therapist, you can acknowledge the humanness of this old, common response (in fact, thoughts about wanting to feel better or wanting to get rid of difficult cognitions will probably always be around) and note that while feeling better or more relaxed is sometimes a pleasant by-product of such exercises, that isn't their purpose. Redirect these clients to the intention of the exercise, which is simply observation of and separation from thoughts in an effort to allow greater flexibility in choosing actions rather than reverting to the control agenda or experiential avoidance. In fact, you may choose to revisit a defusion exercise and have such clients include their wishes that the thoughts would disappear in the exercise. Here are a couple of examples of how you might do that, the first addressing thoughts "going away," and the second addressing "feeling better." You can alter both of these scripts to fit individual clients by inserting specific information about their struggle, avoidance, values, and so on.

Thoughts "Going Away"

Therapist: How was that for you? What did you notice?

Client: It was great! I loved having my thoughts disappear.

Therapist: Yes, that's a pretty common reaction to this type of defusion exercise, wanting those old pesky thoughts to disappear. I wonder, though, do you think they're gone for good?

Client: Hmm, probably not.

Therapist: Yeah, it might be nice, but it probably won't happen. And the thought *I wish these thoughts would just go away* will probably stick around too. But remember, it's not really the thoughts themselves that are so much the problem; it's what you do with them. So the purpose of this exercise isn't to try to make your thoughts go away, because as you know from years of experience, that doesn't really work. The purpose is simply to notice the thoughts so that you don't get so wrapped up in them and can make some different choices—choices that are more closely aligned with the things that are most important to you.

Feeling Better

Therapist: How was that for you? What did you notice?

Client: It was great! I feel so much better.

Therapist: It's certainly nice to notice a reduction in your distress after a defusion exercise, and that's not at all uncommon. However, I want you to remember that we aren't trying to control your internal experiences. From what you've told me, when you've done that in the past it hasn't worked out so well. Sometimes it's even made things worse, so we don't want to go back there. Our aim with defusion isn't to control those thoughts and feelings; it's simply to notice them and get some separation so you can make different, more flexible choices—choices that are more closely aligned with the things that are most important to you. So when these exercises make you feel better, that's certainly okay and you can feel free to enjoy those moments. But that may not always happen, and it isn't our purpose.

Defusion Exercises for Stepping Back and Observing

The following section provides exercises aimed at facilitating defusion through stepping back and observing thoughts as separate from the self.

◆ ◆ ◆

FLOATING LEAVES ON A MOVING STREAM
(Hayes, 2005, p. 76–77)

The exercise Floating Leaves on a Moving Stream, often referred to as simply Leaves on a Stream, is probably the best-known defusion exercise for stepping back and observing thoughts. Its imagery can be universally appreciated and applied, and its simplicity makes it appropriate for any client population.

> *Close your eyes and imagine a beautiful, slow-moving stream. The water flows over rocks and around trees, descends downhill, and travels through a valley. Once in a while, a big leaf drops into the water and floats downstream. Imagine you're sitting beside that stream on a warm, sunny day, watching the leaves float by.*
>   (Pause briefly.)
> *Now become conscious of your thoughts. Each time a thought pops into your head, imagine that it's written on one of those leaves. If you think in words, put them on the leaf as words. If you think in images, put them on the leaf as images. The goal is to stay beside the stream and allow the leaves to keep floating by. Don't try to make the stream go faster or slower. Don't try to change what shows up on the leaves in any way. If the leaves disappear, if you mentally go somewhere else, or if you find that you're in the stream or on a leaf, just stop and notice that this has happened. File that knowledge away and then once again return to the stream. Watch a thought come into your mind, place it on a leaf, and let the leaf float downstream. Continue for the next few moments, just watching your thoughts float by.*

◆ ◆ ◆

WATCHING THE MIND-TRAIN
(Hayes, 2005, p. 66–68)

Watching the Mind-Train is a classic defusion exercise for stepping back and observing thoughts. What's particularly nice about this exercise is that it incorporates emotions, physical sensations, and urges to act, in addition to thoughts.

> *Imagine that you're standing on a bridge over a railway, gazing down at three sets of train tracks. On each set of tracks, a mining train is slowly moving away from you.*

Each train is composed of a string of little cars carrying ore. Seemingly endless, all three trains chug slowly along underneath the bridge.

As you look down, imagine that the train on the left carries only the ore of things you notice in the present moment. That ore is composed of sensations, perception, and emotions. It carries things like the sounds you hear, the sweaty palms you feel, the skipped heartbeats you sense, the sadness you notice, and so forth. The middle train carries only your thoughts: your evaluations, predictions, self-conceptualizations, and so on. And the train on your right carries your urges to act: the pull to avoid and look away, efforts to change the subject, and so on. Looking down on these three tracks is a metaphor for looking at your mind.

Now think about something you've been struggling with lately, then close your eyes and picture the three tracks. Your job is to stay on the bridge, looking at the trains. If you find your mind has gone somewhere else, or if you discover that you're in one of the cars chugging down the railroad track and struggling with its content, such as a judgment that you'll never amount to anything or a belief that nothing good can ever happen to you in the future, this can be a very important moment. In fact, it's a major purpose of the exercise. When this happens, as it will, notice what just hooked you. File that away and then mentally return to the bridge over the tracks and look down once again.

When you're able to stay on the bridge, your experience will look like a variety of thoughts, feelings, and urges to act moving along underneath you, separate from you. If you disappear into the content, getting fused with thoughts, feelings, and urges, your experience will look like a hopeless mess. See if you can stay on the bridge, watching your thoughts, feelings, and urges chug by on the cars below. If you leave the bridge, just notice what happened and then return to your spot over the tracks. Spend the next few minutes noticing what comes up for you.

◆　◆　◆

KICKING SOCCER BALLS
(John Robert-Clyde Helmer, 2013)

Kicking Soccer Balls is a perfect exercise to use with clients who are athletic or play sports, especially those who like soccer. It can also easily be modified to reference other sports to fit the interests of a particular client.

If you're willing, start by closing your eyes. Take a moment to allow yourself to sink into the chair or couch and just breathe.

Now picture yourself on a soccer pitch of your liking. It can be a famous soccer pitch, like Liverpool's Anfield, or one that you enjoyed playing on when you were younger. The specific soccer pitch doesn't matter; just choose one that you can picture in your mind's eye. As you're imagining yourself on this soccer pitch, keep breathing.

Take a moment to imagine that you're at the touchline near the goal, facing the large open field, and there's a soccer ball right next to you. As you reach down to pick it up, you notice something written on it. As you begin to focus on it, you notice a thought that's distressing to you. When you can see that thought clearly on the ball, place the ball back on the goal box line, keeping your focus on the thought as you step back to kick it. Now run up to the ball and kick it off into the distance, watching it travel from where you're standing. As you watch the ball travel off into the distance, take another deep breath.

Now return to the touchline and do this with another ball and another thought. It might be the same thought popping back up again, or you might notice a different thought showing up. (Repeat the exercise with as many fused thoughts as desired.)

Figuring out the sport and team a client likes prior to using this exercise is recommended. As mentioned, this exercise can be used with any type of sport. If the client is a golfer, for example, he can place the ball with the distressing thought on a tee and hit it off the tee. Football players can punt or throw the ball into an end zone. If you know the client likes a particular team, he can imagine being in the stadium or arena of that team.

◆ ◆ ◆

BOAT ON THE WATER

(Benjamin Bryan, 2013)

For the exercise Boat on the Water, clients don't actually place thoughts and feelings onto objects; rather, they experience thoughts and feelings as rising and falling, coming and going, in much the same way a boat rises and falls on waves in the water.

Close your eyes and imagine you're on a boat in the ocean. Imagine using all of your senses as you float along on this boat. Smell the ocean air. Feel the sun on your skin.

Picture the horizon meeting the ocean. Feel the boat swaying gently beneath you. Gentle waves begin to hit the boat, and you feel the boat rise and fall as you hear each small wave hit. Almost as soon as you realize a wave has come, it has passed, and it's not long before another comes along. Sometimes the waves come quickly and powerfully, then pass. Sometimes the waves are so big that they are all you can see and feel until they too pass.

As the waves continuously go past you, some big, some small, feel each one. And as you do, try to notice any thoughts and feelings that arise as well. As you notice these internal experiences, see if you can just ride the waves, allowing the thoughts and feelings to rise and fall, come and go. Stay on the boat, and if you notice that you've been swept overboard into the water, just notice that this has happened, climb back into the boat, and continue to ride the waves.

Defusion Exercises for Deliteralizing Language

The following section provides scripts for exercises aimed at facilitating defusion by connecting with words as sounds and detaching from the literal meaning of the language.

◆　◆　◆

PICKLE, PICKLE, PICKLE
(adapted from Titchener, 1916, p. 425)

The exercise Pickle, Pickle, Pickle and the many other similar exercises described in the literature (including Milk, Milk, Milk in Hayes et al., 1999) are intended to divest meaning from words, in this case beginning with the word "pickle." Of course, this can be done using any word, and is ultimately most helpful with content taken from the client's typical internal experiences (e.g., "failure," "danger," or "I'm weak"). We recommend beginning with the more benign word "pickle" and then following up with a word that's personally evocative for the client. You'll interact with the client throughout this exercise. Be sure to give her a chance to answer the questions seeded throughout the script.

I want you to say the word "pickle." What shows up?... What does it look like?... (If the client doesn't use much detail, you can follow up by asking her to describe the color, texture, and so on.) *If you imagine smelling the pickle, what shows up?… How does it taste?… How does it feel in your mouth and between your teeth?*

Now, are there any pickles in this room? (Clients typically say no.) *Yet, simply because you thought the word "pickle," you can now see, feel, smell, and taste it. You even had some reactions like _____.* (Use the client's experience here. Did she say she loves or hates pickles? Did she notice salivation?) *This is what happens with language: the words that we think bring a whole lot more to the table than just the words themselves.*

Now I want you to try something with me. Let's both say the word "pickle" out loud, over and over, as fast as we can, until I say to stop. (Do this for about a minute, periodically encouraging the client to keep it up, go faster, get louder, and so on.) *Okay, stop. What happened to the pickle?* (Give the client a chance to answer. Universally, people report that after saying the same word over and over, the word becomes meaningless.) *After saying it over and over, all of that other stuff fell away. "Pickle" became just a word or even a silly sound. So how might this apply to the thoughts in your head?*

Spend some time discussing defusion, and then repeat the exercise with difficult content that fits the client's experience—for example, saying "failure" or "ugly" over and over again for about a minute.

◆　◆　◆

FOR S/HE'S A JOLLY GOOD _____
(Ken Davis, 2013)

The For S/he's a Jolly Good _____ is best used when a client has become fused with a particular self-label, such as "I'm a failure," "I'm an imposter," "I'm a poser," or "I'm an alcoholic." Similar to the exercise Pickle, Pickle, Pickle, above, this exercise helps strip the strength and meaning out of the literal language. An example script follows. Use it as a template and change the content to match a client's experience.

Since breaking up with your girlfriend, you seem to be particularly fused with a thought that's making it difficult for you to move forward with dating other women. You've mentioned that you've called your ex a few times and followed what she's been up to on her Facebook page, and that these behaviors have led you to this idea that you're a stalker. You said to me, "What is any girl going to want with an obsessive stalker?" Your powerful belief in this idea is keeping you from pursuing valued relationships. So I want you to try something with me. Do you know the song "For He's a Jolly Good Fellow"? I want you to sing this song with me, only instead of "fellow," we'll sing this song about you and use the word "stalker." So our version will be "For He's a Jolly Good Stalker." Are you willing to do this exercise?

Sing the song together with enthusiasm (the original lyrics appear below), and follow up with a discussion about what happens to the client's thoughts and feelings as he sings this song about his conceptualized self. He should notice that the meaning falls away and the thought becomes less powerful.

American Version

For he's a jolly good fellow, for he's a jolly good fellow

For he's a jolly good fellow (*pause*), which nobody can deny

Which nobody can deny, which nobody can deny

For he's a jolly good fellow, for he's a jolly good fellow

For he's a jolly good fellow (*pause*), which nobody can deny!

British Version

For he's a jolly good fellow, for he's a jolly good fellow

For he's a jolly good fellow (*pause*), and so say all of us

And so say all of us, and so say all of us

For he's a jolly good fellow, for he's a jolly good fellow

For he's a jolly good fellow (*pause*), and so say all of us!

◆　◆　◆

SAY IT IN ANOTHER LANGUAGE
(Matthieu Villatte & Jean-Louis Monestès, 2013)

The exercise Say It in Another Language, first published in French (Monestès & Villatte, 2011), allows clients to perceive how the words in thoughts can narrow their flexibility and drive unhelpful or destructive behavior. It helps clients distance themselves from thoughts by noticing their arbitrariness. It's best to choose a thought from the client's own experience—one that narrows his flexibility. For example, we've chosen *I must drink to feel good*. You need to prepare for the exercise before the session because it's safer to use a language that most people don't speak, such as Icelandic or Gaelic. It isn't necessary to offer a perfect translation, so it's fine to use one of the free translators available on the Web.

> *Therapist:* I'm going to show you a sentence written on this sheet of paper, and I'd like you to read it out loud if that's okay.

Show the client the sentence written in another language—again, ideally one the client doesn't know. In this example, the therapist shows the client a Chinese translation of "I must drink to feel good": *Woqi a nwàn yingg a i he shut, yàobùrán wo juédé bù sh u fu.*

> *Therapist:* Go ahead and try reading this sentence for me.

> *Client:* I'm not sure I know how to pronounce it, but okay. *Woqi a nwàn yingg a i he shui, yàobùrán wo juédé bù sh u fu.*

> *Therapist:* Could you tell me what you feel when you read this sentence?

> *Client:* Not much. It doesn't mean anything to me. It's just sounds that don't evoke anything particular.

> *Therapist:* Do you feel like doing something in particular as you read it?

> *Client:* No, nothing special.

Then write the same sentence in English and show it to the client.

> *Therapist:* What about this sentence? Can you read it out loud too?

> *Client:* "I must drink to feel good." Is that what the other sentence meant?

> *Therapist:* Yes, in fact, it's exactly the same sentence, except that the other was written in Chinese. What did you feel this time, reading the second sentence?

> *Client:* It bothers me. That's what I tell myself all the time.

Therapist: When you have this thought, it seems like it's very difficult for you not to act on it—a bit like an order that you can't disobey. Is that right?

Client: Yes, it comes as a loop in my head. I feel depressed, and I have to drink to stop feeling that way.

Therapist: Can you notice that it seems impossible not to react to the words of this thought, and yet when you hear it in another language, you don't seem as controlled by it?

Client: It's like when I don't know what it means, it doesn't have the same impact on me, even though both sentences are saying the same thing, just using different sounds.

In this exercise, the aim is to lead clients to have a different experience with the thought. Then they're encouraged to generalize this experience beyond the exercise.

◆ ◆ ◆

DON'T DO WHAT YOU SAY

(Jean-Louis Monestès & Matthieu Villatte, 2013)

The exercise Don't Do What You Say was also first published in French (Monestès & Villatte, 2011). In this exercise, clients are experientially taught to behave independently from their thoughts. Begin by standing face-to-face with the client. You'll engage in a series of actions like clapping your hands, then sitting on a chair, then jumping, and so on. The client's task is to describe your action out loud, starting the sentence with "I must..." and completing it with the action you just performed. For example, if you raise your hands, the client says, "I must raise my hands." While doing so, the client's task is to simultaneously perform a different gesture—anything but the action you just performed. For example, if you sit on a chair, the client would say, "I must sit on a chair," while simultaneously doing something different, like hunkering down, crossing her arms, or standing on one foot.

Do about ten different actions before debriefing this exercise so the client has time to experience how it feels to do something different than what she's saying. This exercise helps clients perceive that it's possible to disobey language, and that there's no intrinsic link between thoughts (language) and actions, even if behaving independent of language seems difficult at first.

Sometimes clients do the exact opposite of the therapist's gesture. For example, if the therapist jumps, the client hunkers down, or if the therapist moves a step forward, the client moves a step backward. Such responses are quite normal, since it's difficult to behave independently from language. However, this kind of response—doing the opposite—still reflects what the client said out loud. Behaving exactly opposite to what she's saying also results in a narrowing of her behavioral repertoire.

When a client behaves this way during the exercise, you can discuss this point with her and explore whether such reactions also happen in her everyday life. For example, does the client systematically urge herself to speak in public in reaction to the thought *I won't be able to speak in front of this group*? While behaving in opposition to one's thoughts can be sometimes seen as an efficient exposure strategy, it's more effective to improve the client's ability to behave according to what's important to her, rather than systematically reacting to her thoughts (whether in keeping with or in opposition to those thoughts). This will improve behavioral and psychological flexibility.

◆　◆　◆

NAME THAT TOON
(Mark J. Stern, 2013)

The exercise Name That Toon is a playful technique for gaining some distance from thoughts. Ask the client to choose a cartoon character he thinks might represent or symbolize how he feels or behaves, and particularly a character he could never take seriously. Using thoughts that are typically sticky for the client (i.e., that prevent psychological flexibility or pull him away from his values), have him imagine these thoughts being spoken in the voice of that cartoon character. For example, a client who's anxious and detail oriented might pick Brainy Smurf because Brainy is always worrying over every little thing, yet the other Smurfs dismiss him and never take him seriously. In this case, ask the client to hear his negative thoughts in Brainy's annoying but comical voice.

The hope is that the client won't be able to take those thoughts seriously. Instead, he will see that it doesn't matter whether they're right or wrong, and that he has a choice about whether to attend to them or not. If you're talented in the impersonation department, you can voice the thoughts out loud for the client.

◆ ◆ ◆

NEWS OF THE WORLD
(Jacqueline A-Tjak, 2013)

News of the World is a great experiential exercise to use in a group setting, but it can be adapted to use with an individual as well. It can be particularly useful with combat veterans or other trauma survivors who tend to be triggered by news stories. You'll need a newspaper to conduct this exercise. Give each group member a section of the newspaper.

I'd like each of you to take your section of the newspaper and choose a headline or story that really speaks to you—something that makes you really feel. Choose a sentence from the article or the actual headline. In a moment, I'll ask you to read it aloud. (Give group members a few minutes to do this, then choose a group member to begin with, addressing that person by name.)

Now _____ , I want you to start reading your line, and as you do so, manipulate your paper in such a way that it becomes like a musical instrument. You might crinkle the paper like this, shake it like this, or maybe tap it like this. (Physically demonstrate each suggestion.)

You can make other suggestions for making music, such as using a pen to hit the paper, rolling the paper into two cylinders like drumsticks and tapping them on a desk or chair, and so on. You can let clients get creative, or if they need help, you can get creative yourself in offering suggestions.

I want you to read that line in a rhythm that matches your instrument, and just keep repeating that line and rhythm. So perhaps something like this. (Demonstrate, then have the first group member begin. Once the rhythm is established, invite a second group member to join in.) *Now _____ , I want you to join in with your line and your instrument. Try to do this so you're somewhat in sync.*

Continue until all group members are involved and the group is "making music" together. Let them continue in this way for a few minutes, then process the experience. People typically notice that the content of the words disappears completely and that the words become just noises, sounds, and maybe even fun. Point out that initially these statements were very powerful, and then ask about how this might translate to the group members' experience of their own thoughts. This can facilitate a new relationship to difficult thoughts (i.e., when thoughts are experienced as just sounds, they lose their power). You might consider repeating the exercise, this time using group members' actual troubling thoughts.

♦   ♦   ♦

BRAIN BINGO
(Jill Stoddard, 2013)

Brain Bingo is an exercise that was specifically designed for use in a group setting. It can be used with internal experiences in general or modified for specific client populations, such as patients with chronic pain or victims of military sexual trauma. (See suggestions for modifications below.) It can also be used to introduce self-as-context as described at the end of the exercise.

Give all group members a bingo card, with B-I-N-G-O written across the top and down the side and twenty-five blank squares in the middle. Also give everyone several small blank index cards. Ask them to write a negative thought on each index card using single words or brief phrases, not full sentences, and sticking with thoughts they typically notice in their own mind (e.g., "failure," "stupid," "not good enough," "alone," "never amount to anything," "fat," "ugly," "alcoholic"). Then have everyone fill in the blank squares on their individual bingo cards with the same or similar words and phrases. You can either allow group members to share what they're writing on their individual cards so everyone can write words and phrases they know will appear during the game, or have them write words and phrases that represent their best guesses given what they already know about their fellow group members. Either is fine, but the former is more likely to result in someone actually getting a bingo.

Collect the index cards and put them in a box, hat, or other container. Next, play bingo by pulling cards out of the box, saying the word or phrase out loud, and having group members mark their cards if that thought is present on it. The first member to mark five in a row in any direction yells "Bingo!" and is the winner. Consider giving a small, inexpensive prize to winners—maybe even a Chinese finger trap, since these are a classic ACT symbol of giving up the struggle for control.

Alternatively, you can change the word "BINGO" to a negative word that fits the client population. In this case, you'd ask group members to supply negative words and phrases specific to their presenting problem. Here are some examples:

PAIN for a chronic-pain group, who might come up with words like "useless," "hopeless," "broken," and "ouch"

RAPE for a military sexual trauma group, who might come up with words like "unsafe," "victim," and "vulnerable"

KILLER or BOMB for a military PTSD group, who might come up with words like "my fault," "should've been me," and "unsafe"

Finally, you can also use this exercise to preview or introduce self-as-context, pointing out that the clients (i.e., their being, identity, or sense of self) are like the bingo card and that this card holds the varying experiences of their thoughts, which exist and change on the surface of the card.

Defusion Metaphors

The following section provides several scripts aimed at facilitating defusion through the use of metaphors.

◆　◆　◆

FLY FISHING
(Richard Whitney, 2013)

The Fly Fishing metaphor primarily targets fusion and defusion, but it also serves as a reminder of the problems that arise when we struggle to avoid internal experiences. In addition, it underscores the fact that the purpose of defusion is to gain more flexibility to move in valued directions.

Have you heard of fly fishing? A good fly fisher knows exactly what the trout are feeding on and ties up flies that imitate those insects. They are so good at this that the trout can't tell the difference. They cast the fly into the stream right in front of the trout, and the trout sees it floating by, buys that the fly is real, bites it, and gets hooked.

Our minds can be like really skilled fly fishers. Our thoughts and feelings are like highly specific flies the mind designs—just the ones we'll bite on. The mind casts them out on the stream in front of us, and they seem so real that we buy them, bite, and get hooked.

Once we're hooked, the more we struggle, the more we behave in ways that drive the hook in deeper and keep us on the line.

As we swim in the stream of life, there are flies floating by on the surface all the time. As we get better at spotting flies and recognizing that we don't have to bite them, we get hooked less often and have more flexibility to swim in the direction of our values.

◆ ◆ ◆

HANDS AS THOUGHTS

(Harris, 2009, p. 20)

Hands as Thoughts is a combination of metaphor and exercise in that it's an active, experiential depiction of fusion and defusion.

Imagine for a moment that your hands are your thoughts. Hold your hands together, palms open, as if they're the pages of an open book. Then slowly and steadily raise your hands up toward your face. Keep going until they're covering your eyes. Now take a few seconds to look at the world around you through the gaps between your fingers and notice how this affects your view of the world.

What would it be like going around all day with your hands covering your eyes in this manner? How much would it limit you? How much would you miss out on? How would it reduce your ability to respond to the world around you? This is like fusion: we become so caught up in our thoughts that we lose contact with many aspects of our here-and-now experience, and our thoughts have such a huge influence over what we do that our ability to act effectively is significantly reduced.

Now once again cover your eyes with your hands, but this time lower them from your face very, very slowly. As your hands slowly descend beneath your eyes, notice how much easier it is to connect with me and the world around you. This is like defusion. As you lower your hands your thoughts don't disappear, but getting some separation allows you to engage more fully and flexibly, freeing you to choose to act in ways that are important to you.

◆ ◆ ◆

THE MASTER STORYTELLER

(Harris, 2009, p. 119)

The Master Storyteller is a metaphor for the mind's ceaseless narrative, including its evaluations, rules, predictions, and so on. Similar metaphors, also originated by Russ Harris, can be used to make the same point. These include a word machine that manufactures a never-ending stream of words, or a spoiled brat who makes all sorts of demands or throws tantrums when it doesn't get its way.

The human mind is like the world's greatest storyteller. It never shuts up. It's always got a story to tell, and more than anything else it just wants us to listen. It wants our full attention, and it will say anything to get our attention, even if it's painful or nasty or scary. And some of the stories it tells us are true. We call those facts. But most of the stories it tells us can't really be called facts. They're more like opinions, beliefs, ideas, attitudes, assumptions, judgments, predictions, and so forth. They're stories about how we see the world, what we want to do, what we think is right and wrong or fair and unfair, and so on. One of the things you and I want to do here is learn how to recognize when a story is helpful and when it isn't. So if you're willing to do an exercise, I'd like you to close your eyes and not say anything for about thirty seconds—just listen to the story your mind is telling you right now.

Spend some time processing this with clients—not debating whether their mind's story is true or untrue, but noticing thoughts that are unhelpful and tend to pull them away from doing things that are important to them.

Once you've used this metaphor in session, you can return to it later by saying things like "It sounds like the master storyteller has a captive audience today!" or "My, my, the word machine is really churning them out today!" This will become a quick shorthand for pointing out fusion when it's happening in session.

Summary

Cognitive fusion occurs when we get hooked by the content of the mind, taking it literally and allowing our actions to be driven by our thoughts, even if these choices are incongruent with our values. Defusion is the process by which we disentangle from that self-talk, either by stepping back and observing thoughts as separate from ourselves, or through the deliteralization of language. These processes don't remove thoughts or discomfort; rather, they create a space from which we can make new, valued choices.

In this chapter, we provided a variety of defusion exercises and metaphors. You can generate many more. Defusion exercises that resemble Watching the Mind-Train (Hayes, 2005, pp. 66–68) or Floating Leaves on a Moving Stream (Hayes, 2005, pp. 76–77) can be developed using any image that allows clients to stand still in their mind's eye while watching an object or objects move past, creating a vessel to contain and observe thoughts. This image can be tailored to specific clients. For example, if you're treating children, you might have them imagine parade floats on the Fourth of July. Adults interested in long-distance running or cycling might imagine being a spectator at a marathon or the Tour de France. The idea is to have clients notice the thoughts that arise and place the thoughts outside themselves, allowing them to step back, separate from the thoughts, and watch the thoughts go by. Any exercise that promotes this sense of separation and observation is a defusion exercise. Likewise, any exercise that facilitates experiencing language as just words or sounds separate from meaning, as in deliteralization, is also a defusion exercise. We encourage you to get creative and try your hand at developing some exercises of your own. This is one of the fun parts of therapy!

◆   ◆   ◆

Metaphors and Exercises Targeting Cognitive Defusion

Metaphors and Exercises in This Chapter

- Floating Leaves on a Moving Stream
- Watching the Mind-Train
- Kicking Soccer Balls
- Boat on the Water
- Pickle, Pickle, Pickle
- For S/he's a Jolly Good _____
- Say It in Another Language
- Don't Do What You Say
- Name That Toon
- News of the World
- Brain Bingo
- Fly Fishing
- Hands as Thoughts
- The Master Storyteller

In addition, the following exercises and metaphors, available in the sources cited, also target cognitive defusion.

Other Exercises

- And/Be Out Convention (Hayes et al., 1999, p. 167)
- Contents on Cards (Hayes et al., 1999, p. 162)
- Describing Thoughts and Feelings (Hayes, 2005, pp. 78–79)
- Identifying Programming (Hayes et al., 1999, pp. 143–144)
- Labeling Your Thoughts (Hayes, 2005, pp. 75–76)
- Milk, Milk, Milk (Hayes et al., 1999, pp. 154–156)
- Physicalizing (Hayes et al., 1999, pp. 170–171)
- Reasons for Depression (Zettle, 2007, pp. 102, 176, 245–246)
- Revocalization (Zettle, 2007, pp. 98–99)
- Soldiers in the Parade (Hayes et al., 1999, pp. 158–162)
- Taking Inventory (Zettle, 2007, p. 99)
- Taking Your Mind for a Walk (Hayes et al., 1999, pp. 162–163)
- Your Mind Is Not Your Friend (Hayes et al., 1999, pp. 151–152)

Other Metaphors

- Bad Cup (Hayes et al., 1999, pp. 168–169)
- Finding a Place to Sit (Hayes et al., 1999, pp. 152–153)
- Flat Tire (Zettle, 2007, p. 103)
- Two Computers (Walser & Westrup, 2007, pp. 92–94)
- We Are Fish Swimming in Our Thoughts (Hayes, 2005, p. 55)

CHAPTER 5

PRESENT-MOMENT AWARENESS

with Sheeva Mostoufi and Jessica Gundy Cuneo

The ACT process of present-moment awareness has roots in what is traditionally known as mindfulness. A definition of mindfulness can be found in early Buddhist scriptures such as the Abhidhamma Pitaka (Kiyota, 1978). In the Pali language (the language of the earliest Buddhist scriptures), it is known as *sati*, a word meaning "to remember" (Analayo, 2006). More specifically, *sati* is a state of seeing internal and external experiences, including thoughts, sensations, emotions, actions, and surroundings, as they truly are in the present moment (Chiesa & Malinowski, 2011). A commonly cited modern definition is "paying attention in a particular way: on purpose, in the present moment, and nonjudgmentally" (Kabat-Zinn, 1994, p. 4).

Defining Mindfulness

In the Western world, mindfulness is rooted in specific meditation techniques (Rapygay & Bystrisky, 2009), including concentrative and mindfulness meditation, or open awareness (Chiesa & Malinowski, 2011). The concentrative type involves focusing attention on a specific object and is believed to have a more calming effect on the mind (Cahn & Polich, 2006). In contrast, mindfulness meditation involves an open, nonjudgmental awareness of internal and external experiences, which is considered a more active experience (Brown &

Ryan, 2004). In the Zen meditative tradition, both forms of meditation are valued, and students are first taught to practice concentration over time before beginning to practice open awareness, since developing sustained attention requires practice (Brown & Ryan, 2004). Both types of meditation—concentrative and open awareness—have been integrated into modern definitions of mindfulness. The practice of mindfulness in general is similar to the stance taken in open awareness meditation and is characterized by an orientation of curiosity, openness, and acceptance toward each aspect of present-moment experience.

All of that said, mindfulness remains difficult to define because it's hard to differentiate whether its components are descriptions of mindfulness or outcomes of it (Brown & Ryan, 2004). However, regardless of problems with definition, mindfulness is often considered more a state of mind, as well as a set of skills that can be improved with ongoing practice (Bishop et al., 2004).

Mindfulness and Present-Moment Awareness in ACT

Within ACT, the inclusion of mindfulness creates a different orientation than that in many other psychological approaches. Rather than being goal-directed and attempting to control a conscious experience, such as evaluating a thought or interpreting a problem, ACT utilizes mindfulness to help people monitor their conscious experience through present-moment awareness, and to help them do so from an open and accepting stance, which is engendered through acceptance, defusion, and self-as-context techniques (Wilson, Bordieri, Flynn, Lucas, & Slater, 2011). As discussed in chapter 2, within ACT, mindfulness is conceptualized as a combination of these core processes (Wilson & DuFrene, 2009), with present-moment awareness being one of the building blocks that supports these mindful processes. Together, these strategies are used to increase psychological flexibility, or the ability to generate varied responses when faced with a problem or obstacle (Zettle, 2007).

Present-moment awareness is the process of bringing flexible and deliberate attention to one's experience as it happens (Wilson & DuFrene, 2009). Clients are encouraged to maintain attention on experiences in the moment and to dispassionately observe these experiences, rather than falling into content about events of the past or fears and expectations about the future. Through this process, ACT promotes ongoing nonjudgmental contact with both psychological and environmental events as they occur, strengthening more direct and immediate interaction with experience and undermining the effects of language. The goal is for clients to experience the world more directly so that their behavior is more flexible and consistent with the values they hold. Early on, present-moment awareness exercises can take the form of simple observation of natural acts such as breathing, directing clients to simply notice the rise and fall of each breath. Introducing these exercises early in treatment can be helpful in several regards: building sustained attention and awareness over time, setting the stage for sophisticated present-moment awareness strategies, and orienting clients to the more complex strategies used to address acceptance, defusion, and self-as-context.

Introducing Mindfulness

Mindfulness has garnered a lot of popular attention as a path to stress reduction and greater enjoyment of life, in large part thanks to self-help literature. In addition, mindfulness techniques in combination with cognitive and behavioral interventions are being used increasingly often in psychotherapy. As a result, many clients may be familiar with at least the common understanding of mindfulness. Some clients may dismiss it as "new age" or inconsistent with their religious beliefs. Therefore, it's important to check in with clients about their previous experiences with mindfulness and to identify any myths or misconceptions that might prevent them from engaging with the practice within ACT. This provides an opportunity to dispel any misunderstandings, define present-moment awareness and mindfulness, and provide an ACT-consistent rationale for why it might be helpful. After all, in ACT, mindfulness is about building attitudes of openness, acceptance, and commitment to living life more consciously, and not just doing specific exercises.

There are several ACT-consistent benefits to practicing mindfulness that you can outline for clients when introducing ACT's general approach to therapy. Perhaps most importantly, ongoing mindfulness practice, including present-moment awareness, can help them recognize the transient nature of all experiences from one moment to the next. This recognition of the flow of experience can help build tolerance for disturbing thoughts, emotions, and bodily sensations, such as anger, anxiety, and stress. Nonjudgmental present-moment awareness can also help them cope with these experiences without the added suffering of struggling against them. Similarly, mindfulness can facilitate greater acceptance of the challenges of life and painful memories. As an added benefit, the sustained attention and concentration cultivated in mindfulness practice can help bring focus to all other activities and areas of life. In short, in the

ACT approach, mindfulness practice helps clients become aware of regrets about the past, worries about the future, anxiety, fear, and other unpleasant internal experiences in an accepting manner, ultimately enabling them to identify their values and engage in committed actions in a more present and flexible way.

Mindfulness and Relaxation

In discussing the benefits of present-moment awareness and other mindfulness techniques with clients, you need to be clear about the distinction between mindfulness and relaxation. Clients often report feeling relaxed after a mindfulness exercise and may confuse mindfulness with relaxation or think relaxation is the goal. It's important to clarify that although feelings of calmness or relaxation may sometimes arise, especially with certain mindfulness practices, relaxation is simply a by-product and not the goal. Rather, the peacefulness they may experience through mindfulness is more about finding peace with all aspects of experience: the positive, the negative (including moments of suffering), and the neutral. When clients report feeling relaxed following a mindfulness exercise, remind them that this is a by-product of the practice, not the aim or goal.

Other Considerations Regarding Mindfulness

Aside from possible misconceptions and misunderstandings about mindfulness, there are several other considerations to keep in mind as you work with clients to build this skill. For example, in many mindfulness exercises clients are asked to close their eyes, yet some clients, especially trauma survivors, may have difficulty doing so because they feel unsafe. Also, although building skills in present-moment awareness requires practice both in and out of session, some clients may have difficulty incorporating mindfulness into their daily activities, and some may be reluctant to do anything other than guided exercises in session. In short, you and your clients will need to work together to choose strategies that fit the client's circumstances and to adapt the practices as needed. Here are some recommendations that can be helpful in maximizing clients' benefits from mindfulness exercises:

- Engage clients in adapting the exercises to fit their needs and circumstances. For instance, it might be helpful to shorten guided exercises, especially initially, or to allow clients to practice with their eyes open. For some clients, present-moment awareness may involve regular daily activities, such as walking, eating, or making coffee. This approach may be especially helpful for reluctant or resistant clients.

- Encourage ongoing practice. As with learning any skill, developing present-moment awareness requires repetition. You might wish to include a brief present-moment awareness exercise at the beginning of each session, both to build the practice and to give clients a range of exercises to practice independently.

- To help ensure regular home practice, clients might choose a specific time of day or a certain daily activity as a reminder to practice. Monitoring forms can also be helpful, providing guidance about homework assignments and creating a more structured home practice. Two examples of monitoring forms are provided in the appendices. Clients can use the Mindfulness Diary (appendix A) to monitor their experiences with various self-guided exercises. The ACT Thought Record (appendix B) is a useful tool later in the therapeutic process and helps bring acceptance, present-moment awareness, and values processes to bear on clients' mindfulness practice in day-to-day situations.

- Encourage clients to experiment during home practice. This can help them figure out what's most helpful in terms of the content of mindfulness exercises and the timing of practice.

- Keep an eye out for opportunities to practice present-moment awareness in session. Aside from specific therapist-guided mindfulness exercises, there are ample opportunities in session to help clients contact their experiences in the present moment, especially when discussing painful emotions or memories. At such times, clients can be oriented to what they're experiencing in the present moment, including feelings, thoughts, and bodily sensations.

Present-Moment Awareness Exercises

Although the concept of being present to ongoing experience is emphasized throughout all ACT interventions, specific exercises can be used to build the practice of present-moment awareness. The general approach to these exercises is to choose an object of attention, such as the body or breath, and make an effort to maintain attention on that object. Clients are instructed to notice when thoughts and feelings take their attention away and to gently bring their attention back to the object. These awareness exercises can be expanded to help build a deepened sense of mindfulness that includes awareness of the many aspects of the object and the experience of interacting with the object, as well as the thoughts and feelings that show up in relation to the object and experience. Present-moment awareness techniques typically come in the form of exercises, not metaphors. The exercises below are designed to build present-moment awareness, sometimes in conjunction with strategies that address acceptance, defusion, and self-as-context.

◆ ◆ ◆

MINDFUL WALKING
(Niloofar Afari, 2010)

There are many variants of Mindful Walking, most having their origins in Buddhist teachings. Walking meditation is also often used in other interventions, such as mindfulness-based stress reduction (Kabat-Zinn, 1991), and has been adapted previously for ACT (e.g., Silent Walking, in Hayes, 2005, p. 109; Kiss the Earth with Your Feet, Walser & Westrup, 2007, pp. 164–165). The object of these exercises is typically to focus attention on the activity of walking. The version presented here emphasizes changing the pattern of walking. It can be modified to incorporate awareness of aspects of the external environment, such as temperature, brightness, sounds, and surroundings, as well as internal experiences, such as thoughts and feelings. The basic structure of this exercise also can be used with any other activity. As with all exercises, be sure to allow enough time for the client to fully experience it (typically up to ten minutes), and leave ample time afterward for the client to reflect on this exercise and share about his experience during the exercise.

> *Here's an exercise that's a way to focus your attention and bring awareness to your experience of walking. There's no pass or fail at this exercise. Whatever you experience is just right. If you find your mind wandering and being pulled away from the present moment and the experience of walking, just gently bring yourself back to the sound of my voice and the walk. Remember that being pulled away and coming back is an important part of learning mindfulness.*
>
> *Close your eyes, get settled into your chair, and take a few deep breaths. Notice how your body fits into the chair. See if you can notice the sensations in your back and legs in the places that are in contact with the chair. Bring your attention to your*

feet and the feeling of your feet resting inside your shoes. You can wiggle your toes and see what it feels like to have your toes rub against each other.

Now I want you to put your feet firmly on the ground and, keeping your eyes closed, slowly stand up, noticing the movements of your body, the sensations in your legs as they pull you to a standing position, and the feelings of pressure in your ankles and feet. Go ahead and take a few deep breaths as you stand there.

Now open your eyes and lift your right leg to begin to walk. Step forward and let your right foot touch the ground. Notice the sensation of your foot hitting the ground and the feel of the ground beneath your feet. Are you stepping on the ground hard or lightly? Are you stepping on your heel first, the ball of your foot, or your toes? Are you stepping on the inside of your foot or the outside?

Now lift your left foot and notice your weight shifting onto your right foot. Notice the process of moving your legs. Which muscles tense or relax as you move? As you step with your left foot, again notice whether you return your foot to the ground heel first, ball of the foot first, or toes first. Continue to walk in the same manner, noticing the sensations in your body as you continue to walk. You may find yourself distracted by what you see as you walk, or your mind may wander. You may find that your thoughts and feelings take you away from the walking. If this happens, gently bring yourself back to the sound of my voice and the sensations in your legs and feet as you walk.

Now I'd like you to take a minute to experiment. Lift your legs higher as you walk, noticing the sensation in the muscles of your buttocks, legs, and feet. Notice if your body moves from side to side as you shift your weight from one side to the other. Are you stepping on the ground hard or lightly? With each step, are you stepping on your heel, the ball of your foot, or your toes first? Are you stepping on the inside of your foot or the outside?

Now walk very slowly, noticing the deliberateness of your movements and each step. Does your body struggle to balance itself? Notice the motion of each foot. Do you step from heel to toe or from toe to heel?

Now that you've walked slowly for a few steps, walk faster, noticing the pace of your steps and the sensations in your legs and feet as you walk.

As we come to the end of this exercise, I'd also like you to notice your ability to choose how you walk. You can walk slowly or quickly. You can choose the height of each step, and you can choose the direction in which you walk. Go ahead and slowly take your last step and come to a stop, resting comfortably where you stand. Take a few deep breaths and bring your awareness back to the room.

◆　◆　◆

OBSERVING THOUGHTS

(Megan Thompson Kates, 2013)

The Observing Thoughts exercise takes the present-moment awareness that's typically practiced with the breath and applies it to thoughts. It has its roots in mindfulness meditation but has been adapted to address the ACT processes of present-moment awareness, defusion, and self-as-context. When conducting this and other meditation-like exercises, it's important to use a soft, gentle voice, preferably guiding the exercise while paying attention to the client's reactions, rather than reading from the script. Additionally, include pauses throughout the exercise to allow time for the client to experience what shows up. This exercise typically takes ten to fifteen minutes.

In this exercise, we're going to spend some time in observation. Go ahead and close your eyes, get settled into your chair, and take a few deep breaths. Alternatively, you can get settled into your chair and find a point on the wall to softly focus your eyes on.

Begin by settling into the moment and into your body, taking note of the sensations of your feet planted on the ground and the sensations of the chair supporting your body…allowing these sensations to bring you into the moment…into the space you are already in. By attending to these sensations, you are inviting your attention—your mind—to join you and join your body here in the present moment.

Take a moment to become aware of your breath and the gentle movement in and out as air is exchanged in your nose, mouth, and lungs. You can note the sensation in your belly or in your chest as this gentle movement of air creates a rise and fall. Simply allow the noticing of sensations to be an anchor point, something to which you attach the attention of your mind. And now see if you can notice the movement of your mind as you're observing sensations, with no need to change or do anything about them. See if you can observe the activity of the mind becoming more evident. Begin to notice the movement of thought and the movement of the thinking mind. As you find this one point of attention, simply allow the thoughts to come and go, much as you did with the breath. Simply sit with them, much like we observed the breath.

As a thought arises, take the stance of an observer, finding that place of being, watching, simply observing thought. Take a moment now and simply notice that the thought has arisen. There's no need to change, judge, or modify the thought. Simply notice that thought. You can notice the features of the thought, much like you noticed sensations of the breath, noticing if the thought has a tone, perhaps heavy, or dark, or light. Is it moving quickly or slowly? Is the thought bringing you to the future or the past? Simply notice the texture, the tone, the feel of the thought and see what it's like to simply observe the movement of the thought as it rises and as it moves. Allow the breath and sensation in your body to be an anchor to which you can return. Simply noticing, watching…without judgment…with curiosity…and with acceptance that the mind gives rise to thought and you observe the thought, just as you observe the breath and sensations.

Thoughts arise like bubbles or clouds, passing and you watch. There's no need to follow one particular thought or get caught in the rush or the momentum. Simply notice the moment, the arising, just as the breath spontaneously rises and falls without requiring that we do anything. And then, when a thought arises, as it's likely to do, see if you can notice that thought for exactly what it is, arising in this moment. Again, notice the features of the thought, much like you noticed sensations of the breath, noticing the tone…the texture…the speed…the direction…the feel…simply observing the movement of the thought as it rises and moves. Allow the breath and sensation in the body to be an anchor to which you can return. Simply noticing, watching… without judgment…with curiosity…and with acceptance that the mind gives rise to thought and you observe the thought, just as you observe the breath and sensation.

Now allow yourself to come back to the breath. Notice the movement of air, chest, belly, and wherever the sensations are most notable for you, allowing that to become the focus of your attention. Take a few deep breaths, inviting in a slightly deeper breath with each inhalation. Notice how the air completely fills your lungs, and then you push it out completely with each exhalation…breathing in and out. Notice the sensations in your feet as they rest on the ground and the sensations in your back where it touches the chair. As you prepare to bring your awareness back into this room, you can offer yourself some gratitude, perhaps for taking time today to be in the present moment with your thoughts, for practicing observing, for choosing to take the stance of simply taking note of your own experience. And when you're ready, you can open your eyes and come back into the room.

◆　◆　◆

THE BAG OF CHIPS
(Fiona Randall & Elizabeth Burnside, 2013)

The exercise the Bag of Chips (which originated in Britain as the Crisp Packet) is a group exercise designed primarily to bring clients in contact with the present moment.

However, it also has elements of acceptance and self-as-context, since client reactions appear to be a function of their relationship to the sound and not the sound itself.

Invite group members to close their eyes and allow themselves to be open to whatever they hear for the next few moments. Once they've settled into their chairs and have taken a few deep breaths, spend some time walking around the group with a bag of chips, shaking and rustling it to make audible sounds. The clients shouldn't be aware that the object is a bag of chips.

After about one minute of making noise with the bag of chips, ask the clients to open their eyes and to comment on their experience. You can ask them to describe the sounds and sensations they experienced. Often, they report that their experience was either negative ("It sounded like nails on a blackboard") or positive ("It sounded like a waterfall"). These comments can be the starting point for a discussion on the distinction between nonjudgmental awareness and a nearly automatic judgmental stance that moves people away from their experience. Additionally, in processing this exercise, you might encourage clients to make a link between their present-moment awareness during the exercise and bringing awareness to their thoughts, emotions, sensations, and other private events.

◆ ◆ ◆

GOING ALONG WITH THE PROCESS
(Manuela O'Connell, 2013)

The exercise Going Along with the Process uses breathing as a vehicle to target awareness, along with acceptance, defusion, and self-as-context. This exercise is helpful when you want to shift a client's focus from one aspect of an experience to awareness of the whole process. It's especially useful for clients with high levels of anxiety or panic, providing an avenue to expose them to all aspects of the process of anxiety or panic.

> *Get comfortable in your chair and take a few deep breaths. Go ahead and close your eyes if you're willing; otherwise, you can softly focus your attention on a spot in front of you. Notice how your body fits into the chair and how your hands are resting on your lap or the arms of the chair. Notice any sounds, perhaps the ticking of the clock or the hum of the air conditioner. Gently bring your awareness to the physical sensations throughout your body, checking in on your feet, legs, thighs, buttocks, back, neck, arms, hands, fingers, and head.*

Now bring your awareness especially to the changing pattern of sensations that comes with breathing. Focus your attention on the place in your body where you can be in touch with your breathing most strongly, the place where you feel the sensations of breathing most vividly and distinctly. Perhaps that place is in your chest, or maybe it's in your belly. Notice the sensations of movement, just as they are. With openness and curiosity, gently bring your attention to the feeling of breathing and how it moves your body. There's no need to try to control your breath in any way; simply let your body breathe by itself.

Now I'd like you to focus your attention on the mild and subtle sensations of each in-breath as the air comes into your body, allowing yourself to go along with the changing physical sensations of each in-breath. As best as you can, stay in touch with each of the sensations associated with air coming into your body, from the beginning of the in-breath until your lungs are filled to capacity, moment by moment. Explore with openness and curiosity how each moment of the in-breath feels. Is there something new you can find in each moment of the whole process of the in-breath by going along with it? Allow the experience of the in-breath to unfold. Each new in-breath is another chance to explore and investigate these sensations, moment by moment.

Now gently bring your awareness to the sensations of that turning point between the in-breath and out-breath. Is it a moment? Is it a process? How does it feel? Focus your awareness on the mild sensations of that part of the breathing cycle. With each breath you have a new opportunity to allow your attention to settle and explore the sensations associated with the change from in-breath to out-breath. Simply allow that experience to unfold.

Now gently bring your attention to the sensations of the out-breath. Focus your awareness on the out-breath and go along with each of its sensations. As best as you can, stay in touch with each of the sensations associated with the breath leaving your body, from the beginning of the out-breath to the point at which you feel the urge to inhale again, moment by moment. What do you discover by attending to the whole process of the out-breath?

Now, as best as you can, turn your awareness to the turning point between the out-breath and the in-breath and notice the changing patterns of sensations. Connect with that particular moment of each breathing cycle. Be in touch with that moment and let the sensations associated with it simply unfold. Now gently bring your awareness to the whole process of breathing. Follow it moment by moment, going along with the changing patterns of sensations in your body associated with the entire cycle of your breath.

As we come to the end of this exercise, take a moment to reflect on the whole of your breathing cycle from the in-breath to the out-breath and back to the in-breath again. See if you can see that the breathing cycle is like anxiety (or substitute whatever the client is struggling with) or any other process in your life. Like the cycle of breathing, the changing patterns of the sensations of anxiety can unfold moment by moment. You can bring your attention, with openness and curiosity, to the whole of the anxiety cycle, simply allowing it to unfold.

When you're ready, come back to the sound of my voice and into this room. Notice the sounds that are around us and the temperature in the room. Imagine what the room will look like when you open your eyes. Then go ahead and open your eyes.

Be sure to allow some time for clients to reflect on their experiences during this exercise and on breathing as a metaphor for any other experience in life. Clients' responses to this exercise can provide guidance in choosing other exercises with more of a focus on acceptance, defusion, or self-as-context.

◆　◆　◆

RESPONDING TO TRIGGERS
(Jason Lillis, 2013)

The exercise Responding to Triggers was designed for use in weight-loss groups with participants struggling with food cravings. The exercise has some commonalities with urge surfing, an approach often used in the context of mindfulness-based relapse prevention for addiction (Bowen & Marlatt, 2009). While the exercise focuses on bringing awareness to the cravings, urges, thoughts, and feelings that arise when faced with a desired food item, it also touches on the distinction between problem solving in the external world versus the futility of the control agenda with internal experiences. The exercise can easily be adapted for use with individuals, cravings for other substances, and other behaviors.

To begin, pull out a pint of ice cream (or another desired food). Scoop the ice cream into a bowl, then slowly go around the room with the ice cream and let each group member see and smell it. Ask group members what thoughts, feelings, and cravings they experience with the ice cream in front of them. Provide paper and pens and have everyone write some of the thoughts, feelings, and cravings that come up. Then ask them to share some examples. As they offer their examples, label them as thoughts, emotions, or cravings. Make sure to label a few of each so clients can experience the distinctions. You can label them verbally, write them on a whiteboard in three columns, or both. Then, use the following script to explore different ways of relating to cravings, ultimately using the metaphor of a wave to help participants consider the possibility of just experiencing cravings as they rise and fall without acting on them.

One way to avoid external triggers is to literally throw them away. (Throw the ice cream into a trash can.) *Where's the ice cream now? It's no longer in front of you; it's melting with a bunch of trash. We've effectively gotten rid of the trigger.*

What about the thoughts, feelings, and cravings? Can you just throw them away? Have you tried to do this in the past? (Solicit examples, with the goal being to get participants in contact with a control agenda—with trying to change or control their feelings or make them go away.) *And in your outside life, what have you tried for dealing with these thoughts and feelings? What do you feel like you should do or should be able to do with them? How have you tried to deal with them when they show up?* (Elicit a discussion of the limitations of control when applied to internal experiences.) *What if it were the case that we can't simply throw these experiences away when we don't want them? Could we try something different with these internal experiences?*

Now I'd like you to try something else. Take a moment to get present with any urges you may have when looking at that carton of ice cream or any other food you typically crave. Imagine picking it up, putting it in your mouth, and beginning to eat it. Try to taste the food as it enters your body.

Notice what thoughts are going through your mind and the emotions and physical sensations that arise, and breathe. What physical sensations are you experiencing in your body? If you feel overwhelmed by urges and sensations, you can always go back to just observing your breath. Remember that you're making the choice to not act on any cravings to eat that arise right now. Just stay with them and observe what's happening in your body and mind.

As you get in touch with any cravings you have, see if you can drop any struggle you're having with those cravings and just let them be. Imagine that you can expand around your cravings and make room for them inside you without having to do anything about them.

Now imagine that your urge to eat is an ocean wave and that you're a surfer, riding that wave of craving with your breath, using your breath as your surfboard. Your job is to ride the wave of the desire to eat, from the beginning and as it grows, staying with it through the peak of its intensity, keeping your balance while the wave of desire rises, until it naturally subsides. You're riding this wave of desire and staying on top of it rather than being wiped out by it.

Notice the craving with curiosity. When have you really just sat with a craving and looked at it, as opposed to reacting to it? Where do you feel it in your body? With your mind's eye, see if you can simply touch the areas of your body where you feel the craving and trace them in your body.

Continue imagining the presence of your desired food. Now notice how you can simply stay present with this craving instead of immediately reacting to it. Notice the thoughts that pass through your mind and the sensations you're experiencing in your body. Be present with the craving. Try to make room for the craving without giving into it and having to act on it.

◆　◆　◆

BLOWING BUBBLES
(Jessica Gundy Cuneo, 2013)

Blowing Bubbles is an active exercise that's useful for focusing on the present moment while also becoming aware of one's thinking process, practicing letting go, and defusing from thoughts. It's a playful exercise that's especially great for children and adolescents. It can be done individually or in groups. You'll need bubble solution and a bubble wand for each participant. The exercise takes twenty to thirty minutes and is best done outside to allow room for participants to blow bubbles.

Once outside, instruct clients to get comfortable and begin blowing bubbles. If conducting the exercise with one client, blow the bubbles yourself and have the client be the observer. If conducting it with a group, clients can switch from blowing bubbles to being the observers.

Have clients begin the exercise by simply observing each bubble slowly rising and watching it drift away. Whether clients are blowing bubbles or observing them, instruct them to concentrate on each part of their experience. Ask those who are blowing bubbles to pay attention to the process leading up to blowing each bubble (e.g., dipping the wand, inhaling, exhaling). Ask those who are observing to watch the bubbles being formed, rising, falling, and disappearing. Encourage everyone to notice when the mind wanders and then deliberately come back to the exercise. After five to ten minutes of observing the bubbles, ask clients to imagine that each bubble contains a thought, feeling, memory, or physical sensation they're encountering in the moment. Direct them to observe the bubbles with acceptance and awareness of their internal experiences. Continue this process for five to ten minutes.

When debriefing, it's important to point out that this isn't a goal-oriented exercise and that it isn't intended to achieve a certain outcome. While some clients may have a positive reaction, others may notice unpleasant internal experiences. Facilitate a discussion of how the experience is unique for each person, and encourage clients to notice the difference between being fully conscious in sustained moment-to-moment awareness and becoming absorbed in the content of the mind, including personal narratives.

♦   ♦   ♦

VALUE PARADE
(Matthew Boone, 2010)

The Value Parade is adapted from the Label Parade, an exercise originally presented by Walser and Westrup (2007, pp. 126–131); an excerpt of the present modification also appears in a chapter by Boone and Canicci (2013, pp. 73–76). While the original exercise was focused primarily on facilitating self-as-context, this adaptation expands on the elements of awareness of private events and also emphasizes the link to values. The exercise is designed for groups and is suggested for use in the later part of therapy, as it requires a great deal of willingness and can last for nearly the entire session.

In preparation for the exercise, post several signs on 8.5 by 11-inch pieces of paper around the room with each displaying the name of a life domain, such as friends, family, work, school, environment, spirituality, fun, health, and so on. Then begin the exercise by asking group members to split into pairs, with one person in each pair being the speaker and the other being the listener. Give each pair a pile of name badge labels, such as the sticky labels that say "Hello, My Name Is…" Then, give the following instructions to the group.

In this activity, I'm going to ask you to take turns being a speaker or a listener. For the next five to ten minutes or so, the listeners will interview the speakers. If you're the listener, ask your partner about a difficult situation and then see if both of you can explore the various internal experiences that come up around that situation. Speakers, later you'll be sharing some of this information with the whole group, so choose something you're willing to be open about.

Listeners, think of the qualities that the best listeners you know have. See if you can embody those qualities while you gently ask questions of the person in front of you. Try to be curious and compassionate. Notice any urges to problem solve, and don't act on them. Instead, just sit with what you hear and continue to ask questions. As you're asking questions, write each distinct internal experience you hear about on a separate name badge. You might write things like "fear," "I'm going to fail," "Oh no, not again," "guilt," "memory of past difficult situations," "heart beating fast," "heavy feeling," "butterflies in my stomach," "I'm no good at this," and so on. Each individual internal experience goes on a separate label. As you write each one, hand it to the speaker. Speakers, stick these labels on yourselves in visible locations. Listeners, here are some questions you might ask:

> *Describe briefly a difficult situation you encounter where thoughts, feelings, and other internal experiences can get in the way.*

> *What's the first internal experience that shows up—something like a thought, feeling, physical sensation, memory, or image?*

> *Then what shows up?*

> *And then what shows up?*

> *Speakers, keep going until you've described all you can. Then switch roles when I instruct you to do so. I'll be coming around to check in with each pair and assist you if you get stuck. Speakers, if you feel significant emotions coming up while you're talking, name some of those experiences so they can be written on the labels.*

It's best to briefly demonstrate what you're asking group members to do. You can do this with a group coleader or a group member playing the role of the speaker. Ask the questions above, write the private experiences the speaker shares on name badges, and hand them to the speaker to stick on her body. Once you've demonstrated this part of the exercise, ask group members to begin. Allow five to ten minutes before having the dyads switch roles; observe the group to see how involved they are to gauge when to have them switch. It's best to complete this phase of the exercise in twenty minutes or less.

Once all group members have a number of labels attached to themselves, ask them to silently walk around the room and pause briefly in front of the signs posted on the walls.

> *Now I'd like all of you to stand up. Take a moment to become aware of where you're standing and notice what you're feeling right now in this moment. When you're ready, start walking silently around the room, taking a moment to pause in front of each sign posted on the walls.*

The idea is for group members to experience walking toward what's important to them at the same time that they're in contact with and carrying their painful private experiences. After they walk around the room for about ten minutes, ask them to sit down and process the exercise. Clients often talk about the powerful experience of the original conversations, which gave them the opportunity to practice being present with themselves and others and express strong emotions. Additionally, clients typically discuss how hard or easy it is to move toward some signs and not others. In this way, they can metaphorically experience moving toward what they care about while carrying their pain and can also identify areas for committed action.

It can be important for the therapist to engage in this exercise as a participant, to gain an understanding of what group members experience, and to demonstrate that as human beings, we all struggle with the inevitable pain of living. You can do the exercise with a group coleader if you have one. If you don't have a coleader, you can silently create the labels for yourself without explaining what they are to the group.

◆ ◆ ◆

THE DANDELION

(Amber Guzman, 2013)

The Dandelion exercise focuses on present-moment awareness of areas of physical pain or discomfort in the body, but it can be adapted for use with emotional pain as well. The purpose of the exercise is to bring attention to painful internal experiences. Likening painful emotional or physical experiences to the seeds of a dandelion blowing in the wind can foster client willingness to bring attention to these painful experiences and facilitate noticing their ebb and flow.

For this exercise, I'm going to ask you to identify an internal experience that's uncomfortable or that you wish would go away. If you're experiencing anger, fear, anxiety, or sadness, you can often feel it physically somewhere in your body. If you're in physical pain, you can certainly identify a place in your body where the pain is most significant. For now, focus on the most intense area of sensation or suffering in your body.

Begin by gently closing your eyes and finding a position that's as comfortable as possible. Breathe deeply, focusing on the rhythm of your breathing.... As you breathe, identify a place in your body where you're experiencing an uncomfortable sensation or pain. This could be a racing heart, tightness in the chest, tingling in the limbs, pain somewhere in the body, a headache, tension in the head or muscles, stomach pain, or nausea.... Wherever the pain or discomfort is, focus on that area of the body. Imagine that the part of your body where you experience the discomfort is a mature dandelion seed head, round, fuzzy, and covered with white seeds. Imagine a big, fluffy, dandelion where your discomfort is.

Breathe into the area of your body where you feel the pain or uncomfortable sensation. As you breathe in, notice the dandelion representing the discomfort you're experiencing.... And as you breathe out, notice that you blow on the dandelion and the seeds holding your discomfort float around in the wind.

Continue to focus your attention on the area of pain or discomfort, breathing in and out, and with each breath, notice the dandelion seeds holding your inner experience and watch them float by. (Allow five to ten minutes for the client to fully experience this; you may prompt the client one or two times by repeating the above instructions.) *Now, you can gently open your eyes and return to the room.*

◆ ◆ ◆

WILLINGNESS WITH AN AVATAR
(Matthew Boone, 2010)

The exercise Willingness with an Avatar includes elements adapted from Russ Harris's *ACT Made Simple* (2009) and has been published in a chapter on ACT in groups (Boone & Canicci, 2013). It's a playful way of developing new relationships with painful thoughts and feelings and incorporates present-moment awareness, acceptance, defusion, self-as-context, and values in a way that goes beyond the therapy setting.

The alternative to trying to control, change, fix, magnify, or minimize a thought or feeling is willingness. Willingness can be described in a number of ways: as allowing our thoughts and feelings to be as they are, regardless of whether they are pleasant or painful; as opening up and making room for our thoughts and feelings; as dropping the struggle with them; as letting them come and go as they naturally do; or simply as showing up for the present moment.

This can be a little abstract, so I'd like to ask you to do an exercise that can make it more concrete. One useful way to get a sense of what willingness is like is to represent your thought or feeling in an object and act willingly with that object. It sounds a little silly, but it can be very helpful.

Here's what I'm going to ask you to do: I'd like you to come up with an object to represent a difficult feeling or thought you have. It can be a ball, a rock, a stuffed animal, an index card—anything. (A small stuffed animal can be useful because it's hard to fight or suppress something that's cute.)

Over the next week, treat this object—and the thought or feeling—like it's something welcome that doesn't need to go away. Here are some ways you can do that: You can carry it around with you and keep it nearby when you're working or studying, eating meals, going to work or to class, or really doing anything whatsoever. It can be in your bag, on a table next to you, or in your hand.

Occasionally, interact with it in a way that's welcoming and caring. For example, hold it gently like something precious, or keep it next to you while you're working on your computer, like it's your sidekick. If it's a stuffed animal, pet it.

Throughout the week, mindfully notice any urges to reassure, fix, or change your object. From time to time, hold it in your hand and notice that it's distinct from you and not the whole of you, just like your difficult feeling or thought. Notice that your awareness of it comes and goes, just like your feeling or thought. Notice that you can let it just be there, or you can focus on it very intently, just like your feeling or thought.

Treat it like an invited guest. You might even say something like "Come on in, sadness, and have a seat." Remember, you don't have to like it to welcome it. Wherever you keep it, give it space to be.

Keep in mind that being present is neither goal oriented nor intended to achieve an outcome. It's simply being with whatever shows up in the moment. There's nothing fancy here. All we're doing is trying to practice interacting with thoughts and feelings in a different way. Notice that we aren't trying to change your thoughts and feelings; rather, we're trying to change your relationship with your thoughts and feelings. We're building a skill that will allow you to experience a feeling in the moment and also do what's important to you at the same time.

◆ ◆ ◆

MUSIC MINDFULNESS AND DEFUSION
(Levin Schwartz, 2013)

Mindful listening exercises can be used to develop both present-moment awareness and defusion. Listening to music through the lens of ACT can provide a particularly rich experience for clients who value creativity and the performing arts. Music also has the potential to be powerfully evocative, with individuals being susceptible to a wide range of internal experiences when listening to music. It can remind us of past experiences and memories and can also elicit powerful emotions, such as joy or sadness. This exercise facilitates observing the complexity of the internal experiences that arise when listening to music.

This exercise can be conducted with various types of music, and the selections should be chosen thoughtfully. Be mindful of musical selections that have lyrics, as the words can impact clients' experience by taking the mind in many different directions. Here are a few musical selections that often work well for this exercise:

Johann Sebastian Bach, *Orchestral Suite No. 3 in D Major* (BWV 1068)

Ben E. King, "Stand by Me"

Bill Frisell, "Cold, Cold Heart"

George Winston, "Cloudy This Morning"

John Lennon and Yoko Ono, "Happy Xmas (War Is Over)"

Johnny Cash, "Folsom Prison Blues"

Otis Redding, "That's How Strong My Love Is"

Yo-Yo Ma, Mark O'Connor, and Edgar Meyer, "Appalachia Waltz"

Today we're going to do an exercise that's another way for us to observe the place where we can witness our experience gently and without judgment. I'm going to play a piece of music, and I'd like you to pay attention to only the sounds and experiences that are happening in the present moment. To do this, some people find it helpful to zoom in on one instrument and pay attention only to that one instrument. Others find it helpful to attend only to sensations in the body, such as breath, pulse, and other physical sensations. As you listen to the music, I want you to just pay attention to your unique experience. (Allow the client to do this for several minutes on his own.)

As you continue to listen, consider this: The experience of listening to music may provoke many sensations, thoughts, experiences, evaluations, and judgments. This is just what our minds naturally do—this is our mental programming, and it's happening all the time. Notice any thoughts, emotions, evaluations, or judgments you're having about the music. Become aware of how you're currently relating to the music. You may find that reflections of your life story, personal history, cultural experience, or current mood allow you to identify with what you're hearing. As you listen to the music, be mindful of the various layers of experience. (Allow the client to do this until the end of the song.)

(After the song ends, continue processing the experience with the client.) *Now gently bring your awareness to the present moment by hearing the sounds in the room. Notice the sensation of pressure in your body where it makes contact with the chair and the floor. In your mind's eye, picture yourself in the room.* (Describe the room.) *When you're ready, rejoin the room by allowing your eyes to open.*

You can use the handout in appendix C to process this exercise either individually or in a group setting. The discussion can focus on how quickly our inner experiences take us away from contact with the present moment. The following questions are helpful for encouraging clients to share their experiences:

What sounds or physical sensations did you experience in the room?

What thoughts or emotions did you notice as you listened to the music?

What evaluations or judgments did you experience while listening to the music?

What's your story? Did you have a memory while listening to the music?

Summary

ACT is an experiential intervention and relies heavily on exercises that focus clients' attention on the present moment, whether the events and experiences noticed are external or internal. Developing the skills necessary for present-moment awareness is key to engaging clients with their experiences and fostering willingness and values-based action. In this chapter, we presented several exercises that can be used to engender present-moment awareness, with a particular focus on those that emphasize the link to acceptance, defusion, and self-as-context.

In general, many ACT exercises—no matter which core process they target—involve present-moment focus or open awareness, making them useful as mindfulness exercises. For example, the eyes-closed mindfulness version of the Sweet Spot exercise in chapter 7 is a great way to begin a session, especially one that will later turn to values, which is the main focus of the exercise. Additionally, the literature on mindfulness is expansive, both within and beyond ACT. Numerous books and websites provide mindfulness exercises that are ACT-consistent or can be easily modified to fit with the principles of ACT.

◆　　◆　　◆

Exercises Targeting Present-Moment Awareness

Exercises in This Chapter

- Mindful Walking
- Observing Thoughts
- The Bag of Chips
- Going Along with the Process
- Responding to Triggers
- Blowing Bubbles
- Value Parade
- The Dandelion
- Willingness with an Avatar
- Music Mindfulness and Defusion

In addition, the following exercises, available in the sources cited, also target present-moment awareness.

Other Exercises

- Attending to Breathing (Walser & Westrup, 2007, pp. 43–44)
- Be Mindful of Your Feet While You Read This (Hayes, 2005, pp. 114–115)
- Be-Still Mindfulness (Walser & Westrup, 2007, pp. 86–87)
- Be Where You Are (Hayes, 2005, pp. 107–108)
- Body Scan (Walser & Westrup, 2007)

- Breathing Mindfully (Zettle, 2007, pp. 143–144)

- Cubbyholing (Hayes, 2005, pp. 109–110)

- Drinking Tea (Hayes, 2005, pp. 111–112)

- Eating Mindfully (Hayes, 2005, pp. 112–113)

- Mindfully Eating Raisins (Kabat-Zinn, 1991, pp. 27–29)

- Finding-the-Center Mindfulness (Walser & Westrup, 2007, pp. 113–114)

- Gazing at the Clouds (Zettle, 2007, pp. 145–146)

- Just Listening (Walser & Westrup, 2007, p. 68)

- Just Sitting (Hayes, 2005, pp. 116–118)

- Kiss the Earth with Your Feet (Walser & Westrup, 2007, pp. 164–165)

- Listening to Classical Music (Hayes, 2005, pp. 113–114)

- Place of Peace (Walser & Westrup, 2007, p. 142)

- Practicing Awareness of Your Experience (Hayes et al., 1999, p. 179)

- Silent Walking (Hayes, 2005, p. 109)

- Tracking Your Thoughts in Time (Hayes, 2005, pp. 100–101)

CHAPTER 6

SELF-AS-CONTEXT AND PERSPECTIVE TAKING

One of the many normal developmental milestones humans achieve during childhood is perspective taking. We learn by experience the difference between I and you, here and there, and now and then. These verbal relations are deictic, or learned by demonstration (Hayes et al., 1999), because they don't involve objects and can only be shown and understood relative to an observational perspective. In this chapter, we will discuss two perspectives one can take with regard to the self: the conceptualized self, or self-as-content, and the observing self, or self-as-context.

The Conceptualized Self or Self-as-Content

As therapists, we might start the initial therapy session by asking new clients to tell us a bit about themselves and what brings them in to see us. The responses we hear are stories clients have created about themselves: judgments, evaluations, thoughts, images, feelings, rules, memories, physiological sensations, roles, and impulses that comprise their sense of self or what they might call their identity. For example, a client might say, "I'm depressed. I can't work, and my friends don't want to be around me. My family doesn't understand me. I've been different since childhood. I didn't fit in then, and I don't fit in now." In ACT, we call this narrative collection of "I am" statements the conceptualized self.

The interpersonal interactions that weave together the fabric of our experience seem to universally lend themselves to an unavoidable construction of these stories or identities. From a very early age we are asked, "What do you want to be when you grow up?" During job interviews and while dating, others say, "Tell me about yourself." Certain "I am" statements may appear to be benign; for one of us (JS), examples include "I am a psychologist," "I am a professor," "I am a wife," and "I am a mother." However, the same verbal constructions that lead to these seemingly harmless labels can easily draw us into unworkable traps. For example, what if I (JS) have verbally constructed a story that says successful, driven professionals must work long hours, but loving mothers must not work long hours? When taken literally, this story says that I can't be both a successful professional and a good mother! The real problem arises when being a loving mother and a driven professional are both important personal values, but actual life choices are determined by an attachment to the conceptualized self or by the content of the stories (thoughts, feelings, rules, etc.).

Returning to the client example above, if this client is dominated by an attachment to her conceptualized self, she's probably isolating herself from friends, family, and coworkers, even if close connections in these realms are quite important to her. In my personal example, I may sacrifice important aspects of my career, or I might try so hard to be both a good professional and a good mother that I burn myself out and have nothing left. In both cases, the sense of self or identity is defined by the content of the person's thoughts, feelings, images, memories, and stories (i.e., self-as-content), and this conceptualized self becomes the driving force behind behavioral decisions.

Perhaps you've heard clients overidentify with their symptoms or pathology by overtly saying, "This is just who I am," in reference to depression, chronic pain, panic attacks, agoraphobia, or another diagnosis. This is a glaring neon sign for the ACT therapist: *Attachment to conceptualized self needing attention here!* But the setup isn't always so obvious. In fact, attachment to a positively valenced conceptualized self can be equally detrimental. For example, a client who proudly describes herself as kind, generous, and someone who never gets angry will be unlikely to set limits or stand up for herself, even when this is clearly warranted. Thus, it's important to be on the lookout for any "I am" statements—positive, negative, or neutral—because attachment to any of these may result in psychological inflexibility.

Let's take a closer look using another example. Suppose you have a new client who tells you, "I am a police officer." This "I am" statement may initially seem neutral and harmless.

Your client tells you more of his story: "Police officers must always watch their backs…" Attachment to this statement might still seem reasonable when you think of a police officer on duty who values his safety and the safety of his partner and the community he protects.

You uncover a little more: "Police officers must always watch their backs, even when off duty, because you never know what threat might be lurking. Officers must always be tough, ready for anything. We must never show emotion because doing so means showing weakness, and showing weakness means being vulnerable. We must never let our guard down and must never be vulnerable."

As you start to dig, you find out that there's a lot more to this story and the "I am" statement that started it. As you get the whole story, you find a man who has come to you because his wife is about to leave him and his two children feel disconnected from him and oppressed by the limits he places on them. In his life, this police officer acts distant, is unaffectionate, and chooses activities based on his estimation of their safety. He doesn't allow his wife or children to do things or go places that may be the slightest bit risky. As his ACT therapist, you now know that you have a client with an attachment to a conceptualized self that has resulted in an inflexible, unworkable psychological agenda.

In an effort to increase psychological flexibility and move away from this unworkable agenda, you need to shift this client's perspective from the conceptualized self, or self-as-content, to the observing self, or self-as-context, allowing him to experience his life as it is and respond more flexibly.

The Observing Self, or Self-as-Context

While the conceptualized self is made up of the ever-changing content of thoughts, feelings, memories, and the like, the observing self, or self-as-context, is the stable, unchanging perspective from which one thinks, feels, remembers, and so on. Self-as-context refers to a sense of self that transcends the content of internal experiences. In other words, from this perspective we aren't defined by our thoughts, sensations, emotions, and memories; rather, we are simply the crucible that contains them.

Likewise, you, the reader of this book, are separate and distinct from your stories and history in exactly the same way that you are separate and distinct from the words you're reading on this page or the furniture on which you currently sit. Of course, the distinction between your self and your sofa is much easier to observe than the distinction between your self and your internal private events. In ACT, we aim to foster a shift from the conceptualized self to the observing self, or the perspective that there's a self that is observing and experiencing the inner and outer world yet is distinct from the individual's thoughts, feelings, memories, physical sensations, impulses, and roles.

To illustrate this, take a moment to think back to some of the following occasions. Depending on your age, you may not remember them all, but for those you do remember, try to recall them in detail, seeing them from behind your eyes as you were at that time: the day John F. Kennedy was shot, the first *Apollo* moon landing, the explosion of the space shuttle *Challenger*, Princess Diana's death, 9/11, and Michael Jackson's death. Now remember one thing you did during the most recent holiday, seeing it through your eyes as you were at that time. And now become aware of what you're doing right now as you're reading this book. See if you can notice that, across time and despite changes in thoughts, feelings, sensations, memories, and roles, there has been a stable, consistent, unified "you" that has been present behind your eyes, seeing and experiencing the world—a "you" that has held those thoughts and stories but has also been separate from them. It's the "you" that has been you for your entire life.

The ACT process of self-as-context aims to shift clients to this observer perspective, allowing them to experience life as it unfolds. The goal is to reduce attachment to the conceptualized self, creating the flexibility necessary for choosing actions based on values, rather than based on stories about the self. This observer perspective also allows clients to establish a place from which they can safely contact uncomfortable or unwanted internal experiences. That is not to say that taking an observer perspective removes discomfort; rather, the transcendent, stable, unchanging sense of self (the you that has been you from your birth through the present moment) need not be threatened by the content of thoughts or the experience of emotions. The observing self notices thoughts and feelings; it doesn't create them. Therefore, the observing self can't judge or be judged, because all it does is observe things, just as they are, in the present moment.

Let's return to the example of the police officer and imagine that his daughter asks permission to attend a party after her senior prom. If he remains attached to his conceptualized self, he'll probably say no—firmly and without discussion, end of story. Imagine how different his response might be if he could step back and observe his thoughts and feelings about fear, weakness, vulnerability, and protection. Then, rather than getting hooked by his content and allowing it to drive his behavior, he would be able to make a choice in the service of his value of being a loving and supportive father. Interestingly, his answer may still be no, but the interaction with his daughter would probably look much different.

Self-as-Context Exercises

Moving away from self-as-content and toward self-as-context isn't a matter of forming a new identity; rather, it is a matter of forming a sense of self that transcends verbal definitions, as well as space and time. The goal is not to change the story, but to let go of attachment to its content.

Making contact with the observing self must be achieved experientially. The Observer exercise (Hayes et al., 1999, p. 192–196) is a quintessential self-as-context exercise designed to put the client in touch with his bodily sensations, memories, roles, emotions, and thoughts, noticing each of these and then noticing that he is also the one noticing. In this way, the client becomes aware of awareness and develops a sense of self that's separate from internal experiences.

Any mindfulness or defusion exercise will facilitate a sense of being aware of one's own awareness. In fact, any exercise can target self-as-context by simply adding an instruction to "notice who is noticing" or to "be aware that you're noticing" (Harris, 2009, p. 176). This can be done in any context, whether noticing the colors of a rainbow, observing the temperature of the water in the shower, hearing the rhythms in music, or watching thoughts float by. Many seminal ACT exercises can be expanded to include a self-as-context component. For example, the classic Passengers on the Bus exercise (Hayes et al., 1999, pp. 157–158) is often used to demonstrate willingness, defusion, and movement in the direction of valued actions. However, self-as-context can be incorporated into this exercise by including the bus driver as the part of the client who is noticing all of these experiences (Luoma, Hayes, & Walser, 2007).

Of course, exercises specifically targeting self-as-context also exist. Below, you'll find a few of our favorites.

◆ ◆ ◆

TALKING AND LISTENING
(Harris, 2009, p. 177)

The exercise Talking and Listening is a quick yet effective way to help clients experientially achieve the observer perspective. This can be a good place to begin laying the groundwork for self-as-context.

For the next thirty seconds, silently listen in to what your mind is saying. And if your thoughts stop, just keep listening until they start again. (Pause for thirty seconds.)
So there you have it: there's a part of your mind that talks—the thinking self—and a part of your mind that listens—the observing self.

◆　◆　◆

OBSERVING SELF WITH VALUES

(Matthew Boone, 2011)

The exercise Observing Self with Values is an adaptation of the original ACT Observer exercise (Hayes et al., 1999, pp. 192–196). It's designed to help facilitate an experiential sense of self-as-context and connect this to values. Therefore, this exercise should be done after you've already engaged clients in a preliminary discussion about values and what they are and are not. The script here is designed to be used in a group setting but can be easily modified for individual clients. When working with a group, begin by breaking participants into pairs or groups of three. You'll need index cards and pens or pencils.

Today we're going to explore the observing self—a new perspective on who you are and what you think and feel. To do this, we're going to start with values as we've defined them in this group. Values are how you choose to be or act on an ongoing basis.

To start, I'd like you to discuss in pairs what you're like when you're at your best in important areas of your life, such as academics, work, family, friendships, romantic relationships, recreation, creativity, or health. You can also pick areas of life other than those I listed. Paint a vivid picture for your partner. Use verbs and action-oriented adjectives to describe yourself. For example, in the area of academics, you might describe yourself as "hardworking and inquisitive."

Give the group five to ten minutes for discussion. Then bring the entire group back together to discuss the exercise. Ask for a few examples. When group members give examples that might be feelings masquerading as values—words like "patient" or "calm"—remind them that those are feelings, which we don't get to choose, as opposed to values, which we do choose, and invite them to restate them as values, such as acting calm or acting patient. Then give each group member an index card and a pen.

Choose a few words that really capture how you are at your best. Write these down on one side of the card. When you're finished, turn the card over. Don't write anything on the other side just yet. I want you to think of some thought or feeling, or a combination of thoughts and feelings, that gets in the way of you being your best. It might be a judgment about yourself. It might be stress or impatience. Or it might be a fear you have. Feel free to pick something small that you're willing to interact with in a new way today. When you've thought of something, represent it on the card either with words or, if you don't want your neighbor to see it, some kind of symbol, such as an X.

Next, we're going to do an experiential exercise that incorporates mindfulness and visualization. We'll begin with mindfulness. Sit comfortably in your chair with your feet flat on the ground, your hands in your lap or on your knees, and your head and neck erect but not rigid. Hold your card in one hand with the feeling facing up. Allow your eyes to close gently.

Come into this present moment by noticing your breathing. Take a moment to connect with your breathing as it flows in and out of your body. In your mind's eye, watch the rising and falling of your chest and belly.... Notice the physical sensations in your body as you breathe in and breathe out.... As best you can, simply let the breath breathe itself.

Now turn your attention to your body in the chair. Notice the sensations of touch or pressure where your body makes contact with the chair.... Notice the varieties of sensation there. Notice how the rising and falling of your breath also manifests in these places. Now turn your attention to your feet inside your shoes.... Notice the variety of sensations there. Notice how the sensations are different in different places—the balls of your feet, your instep, your heels. Now wiggle your toes a little.

And as you're noticing this, notice who's noticing. There is a you there behind your eyes, watching all this as you experience it...a you that is different from your experience. There is this you, and then there is your experience. I call the part of you that's watching the "observing self." Continue to notice your feet inside your shoes from this perspective for a few moments.

Now turn your attention back to your breath in your body. Notice the rising and falling as you breath in and out. Again, notice who's noticing. There is a you there behind your eyes watching your breath flow in and out...a you that is different from your experience. There is you, and then there is this experience of breathing.... This is the observing self. Continue to watch your breathing from this perspective for a few moments.

Now think of all the roles you inhabit in your life. Imagine yourself in those roles...parent, child, brother or sister, student, worker, colleague, partner, friend, neighbor. (To the extent possible, tailor this list to the clients in the group.) Although you are a bit different in each of these roles, it's still the same you inhabiting all of them.... Notice that.

Now think back over your life and consider how much your body has changed. If we were to look at a picture of yourself when you were a child and compare it to you as you are now, we would see so many differences....Every cell in your body is different *now, yet it is still you. When you said "I" as a child, it was the same "I" you're talking about when you say "I" now.... This is a part of you that has always been here.... This is a part of you that hasn't changed.... This is the observing self.*

Now think back over your life and imagine the millions of experiences you've had.... Imagine the millions of thoughts and feelings you've encountered inside you, coming and going, ebbing and flowing, throughout the course of your life.... Some have been painful. Some have been pleasant. They have always been changing, but you have stayed the same.... You've been there the whole time, watching.... This you is the observing self.

Finally, open your eyes and gaze upon the card in your hand. Imagine that the experience described there is actually in your hand, however you make sense of that.... Feel the weight of it in your hand. Now take a moment to notice who's noticing this.... There is a you there, behind your eyes, who is watching this experience that you're holding in your hand...a you that is different from this experience that you're holding in your hand. This is the observing self.

Now let's return to our conversation as a group.

Participants will have a variety of experiences. As you talk about the experience with the entire group, stress the following points:

> *The observing self isn't the "real" self, but merely a perspective you can take on thoughts and feelings to provide freedom to choose values-directed actions.*

> *Notice that the thought or feeling on one side of the card and the values on the other are two parts of a whole. You can't have one without the other. To do what's important, you also have to have the pain that comes with it. If you take away the pain, you also take away the value.*

◆ ◆ ◆

FUSION WITH SELF-EVALUATIONS
(Luoma, Hayes, & Walser, 2007, p. 118)

The exercise Fusion with Self-Evaluations is aimed at guiding clients to objectively observe self-evaluations (often "I am" statements)—positive or negative—and notice these as just words rather than buying the evaluations as fact. In this way, the exercise facilitates detachment from a conceptualized self. The therapist makes a distinction between description and evaluation. In the example dialogue that follows, the therapist begins by describing a pen, but you can use any ordinary object you have in your office.

Therapist: (*Holds out a pen.*) This pen is white, with black letters and a black cap. The tip is metal and has black ink. Agreed?

Client: Yes.

Therapist: Now, suppose I say this is the best pen in the world. There is no better pen. Agreed?

Client: Well, I don't know. I own a pretty darn good pen.

Therapist: Right. You can see how the description is different from the evaluation. "Best pen in the world" isn't *in* the pen. It's something I'm saying about the pen. It's an evaluation I have about it. It doesn't exist in the pen. And "worthless" is an evaluation that doesn't exist in you. (*Use content that's relevant to the specific client.*) It's just something you say about yourself. It has nothing to do with whether you're whole or not. You are the context for the thought *I am worthless*, nothing more. Having the thought doesn't make it true or not true.

◆　◆　◆

I CAN'T POSSIBLY _____

(Jill Stoddard, 2007)

Attachment to the conceptualized self also often means fusion with reasons. In other words, "Because I am _____ (insert a symptom, role, or story here), I can't _____ (insert a valued action here)." The exercise I Can't Possibly _____ challenges this experientially. It works particularly well with anxious clients who offer many reasons for avoiding people, places, or situations they fear. Begin with a brief discussion of the client's specific struggles.

Therapist: John, a few times you've said, "I really want to be more social, but I'm just too much of an anxious person." Do I have that right?

Client: Yeah, doc. I'm awkward and shy. I just can't do it.

Therapist:	That sounds like a pretty compelling story. Would you be willing to try something with me?
Client:	Yeah, sure. Why not? What have I got to lose?
Therapist:	Great. I appreciate that willingness. Raise your right hand for me. (*Raise your right hand too.*) Now repeat after me: "I can't raise my right hand… (*Give the client a chance to repeat after each sentence.*) I am someone who is completely incapable of raising his right hand…. I cannot possibly keep my right hand in the air…. If I have to keep my hand up here for another second I might die…"

You can continue this with other actions, even trying some silly things like hopping on one foot (assuming the client isn't disabled or injured) or doing the chicken dance and adding thoughts about feeling silly or awkward and not being able to stand the embarrassment. You could even play a modified version of the children's game Simon Says, giving clients the instruction "Simon Says *don't* clap your hands" and having them clap their hands despite this instruction. We encourage you to play with this exercise, adapting it in whatever ways might best suit specific clients.

At the end of the exercise, discuss the ways in which attachment to the conceptualized self creates psychological inflexibility and movement away from important values, often in the form of reason giving. Alternatively, when people are able to see the self as separate from the content of their internal experiences, it becomes possible for them to think one way and act another.

◆　◆　◆

CONCEPTUALIZED SELF ON TRIAL
(Jill Stoddard, 2013)

The exercise Conceptualized Self on Trial was designed for a group setting but can be modified as you see fit. Its aim is to show the lengths to which people will go to defend a conceptualized self and the futility and costs of this battle. It's also a defusion exercise in that playing the role of defender of thoughts inherently creates separation from content. Group members must have a pretty good knowledge of one another for this exercise to be successful, so it's recommended for later sessions.

You'll need a few volunteers. First, ask for a volunteer to have his or her conceptualized self put on trial. Then ask for a volunteer to serve as prosecuting attorney and another to serve as defense attorney. Have the first volunteer generate a great number of "I am" statements—both positive and negative, writing them down and then handing them over to the prosecuting attorney and defense attorney. (This simulates the process of discovery.) Ask the prosecution to argue all the reasons why the "bad" identity is valid and the "good" identity is false. Ask the defense to argue the opposite position. Encourage the attorneys to harness their inner *Law and Order*. They can object ("Speculation!"), request to approach the bench, call witnesses, and so on. The group member whose identity is on trial also serves as the judge and can rule accordingly: "Sustained," "Overruled," "In contempt of court," "Strike that from the record," "Approach the bench," "Meet me in chambers," and so on. Have the remaining group members play the jury. If the group is large, additional members could be called as character or expert witnesses.

Try to have fun with it; the more engaged you get the group members, the more defused the content becomes. When the attorneys make their closing statements and it's time for the jury to deliberate, give them one instruction: that their verdict about who this person is must be unanimous and beyond a reasonable doubt. When all is said and done, it should be impossible for the jury to decide. The takeaway point is that maybe the person on trial is both all and none of these things. And just as a courtroom contains lawyers, judges, and litigants engaged in a sort of battle, we humans have our own internal experiences—thoughts and feelings—and sometimes we get caught up in an internal battle, but that battle is unwinnable. However, we don't have to exist at the level of lawyers and judges; we can be more like the courtroom. We can make close contact with and contain those elements, but we are not the content of our "I am" statements.

Self-as-Context Metaphors

A number of metaphors can be used to illustrate the notion that there is a self who experiences thoughts and feelings yet exists separately from that internal content. The most well-known is probably the Chessboard metaphor (Hayes et al., 1999, pp. 190–192), which compares the battle between chess pieces to the constant battle between "good" and "bad" thoughts and feelings. The crux of the metaphor is in its suggestion to shift from the perspective of the chess pieces to that of the chessboard, keeping in close contact with thoughts and feelings but stepping outside the battle and simply containing the pieces.

◆　　◆　　◆

THE CLASSROOM
(Jill Stoddard, 2013)

The Classroom metaphor uses an approach similar to that of the Chessboard (Hayes et al., 1999, pp. 190–192) to facilitate a shift in perspective from self-as-content to self-as-context. Note that the students, teacher, and classroom scenario can be altered to a team, coach, and field of play; soldiers, commanding officer, and battlefield; sales team, manager, and office; lawyers, judge, and courtroom. If possible, use context that's relevant for the specific client. Anytime you can modify a metaphor to make it more salient for a particular client, we encourage you to do so.

> Imagine a classroom full of students. Some of them are "problem" students who talk back to the teacher, stick gum under the desks, and send text messages when the teacher isn't looking. Some are "good" students who pay attention, get good grades, and suck up to the teacher. Some are "average" students who sit at their desks and go relatively unnoticed. Then there's the teacher at the front of the room who evaluates all the students, telling the problem students to pipe down, pay attention, and be good, and praising the good students and putting gold stars on their papers.
>
> Your thoughts and feelings are like the students in the classroom: some are negative, some are positive, and some are neutral. And there's also a part of you that tends to evaluate your thoughts and feelings. Like the teacher, it probably tries to make the negative thoughts pipe down and attempts to keep the positive thoughts around by giving them a gold star. But there is another part to this metaphor: the classroom that contains the students and the teacher. It's in close contact with them yet also separate from them. It's the context that contains them. So perhaps you aren't the students or the teacher—the thoughts, feelings, or evaluations—but the classroom—the vessel that simply contains those experiences.

♦ ♦ ♦

THE SKY AND THE WEATHER
(Harris, 2009, p. 175)

As with other self-as-context metaphors, the Sky and the Weather facilitates defusion and cultivates the observer perspective, but it also places emphasis on providing a safe place from which clients can make contact with painful thoughts and emotions.

Your observing self is like the sky. Thoughts and feelings are like the weather. The weather changes continually, but no matter how bad it gets, it can't harm the sky in any way. The mightiest thunderstorm, the most turbulent hurricane, the most severe winter blizzard—these things can't hurt or harm the sky. And no matter how bad the weather, the sky always has room for it. Plus, sooner or later the weather always changes.

Sometimes we forget the sky is there, but it's still there. And sometimes we can't see the sky because it's obscured by clouds. But if we rise high enough above those clouds—even the thickest, darkest thunderclouds—sooner or later we'll reach clear sky, stretching in all directions, boundless and pure. More and more, you can learn to access this part of you: a safe space inside from which to observe and make room for difficult thoughts and feelings.

◆ ◆ ◆

THE PRINCE AND THE BEGGAR
(Janina Scarlet, 2013)

The metaphor of the Prince and the Beggar aims to demonstrate the continuity of an identity or sense of self that remains stable even through changing circumstances (e.g., roles) and internal experiences (e.g., thoughts and feelings).

Imagine a prince and a beggar who look exactly alike but who wear different clothes and live in different homes. Imagine that one day they meet and decide to switch places for a day. The prince puts on the beggar's rags, and the beggar dons the prince's robes. The prince walks around the city in foul-smelling clothes and is shoved around like the beggar used to be. The beggar wears expensive clothes and is treated like royalty. The beggar in the prince's clothes is very appreciative of the sumptuous food he's given and readily shares it with other beggars. The prince in beggar's clothes steals bread from a little girl; he feels entitled to take it, after all! He talks down to other beggars and won't eat with them. So while the prince and the beggar put on different clothing and are treated differently by others, the person each truly is remains unchanged.

◆ ◆ ◆

TAKING OFF YOUR ARMOR
(David Gillanders, 2013)

The metaphor Taking Off Your Armor may be particularly useful for clients with a history of trauma who have become attached to a conceptualized self that's guarded and untrusting, yet who value closeness and intimacy in relationships. The goal is to help clients see that the armor no longer fits.

Doesn't it seem as though your early life was such a battle that you had to put on strong armor to defend yourself? You became a knight, constantly at war and therefore keeping your armor on all the time. You got so comfortable in your armor that it was like an extension of your own skin and you kind of forgot you were wearing it. And it really worked. It stopped you from being so hurt.

Look at your life right now. Are you still in a battle with people around you? Could it be that the war is over, but you're still clunking around inside this suit of armor? How free are you to move? What is the armor really costing you? While it's true that keeping the armor keeps you from being hurt, is it also stopping you from really having the feeling of being held, being loved? What would it be like to take off this suit of armor that seems to no longer fit?

◆ ◆ ◆

MUNTU

(Jill Stoddard, 2013)

The Muntu metaphor speaks to a stable sense of self that's separate from the body and its thoughts and feelings. It was inspired by a passage in Barbara Kingsolver's book *The Poisonwood Bible* (1998). You might choose this metaphor for clients who like to travel or who are interested in other cultures or languages.

In the Kikongo language, spoken in the Democratic Republic of Congo, the word for "people" is bantu. *The singular form of this word is* muntu. Muntu, *unlike the English "person," refers not only to a living person, but to beings who have yet to be born, as well as those who have died. Muntu is a transcendent self that persists, stably and unchanged, through prelife, life, and afterlife. The Congolese speak of muntu as a self that exists inside the body but separate from it, looking out through the eyes and simply watching what occurs. This self doesn't get attached to outcomes because it isn't affected by them and it can't die. It's a self that simply transitions from spirit to body and back again.*

This is much like the ACT concept of self-as-context: a stable, unchanging self that transcends the content of thoughts and feelings—a self that experiences and contains these elements but isn't defined by them.

◆ ◆ ◆

THE ANTHROPOLOGIST
(Jill Stoddard, 2013)

The Anthropologist is a brief metaphor that helps illustrate the observer perspective.

Taking the observer perspective is like being an anthropologist, but instead of studying the cultural practices of the people of some far-flung location, such as Attu Island in the Aleutians, you're observing the practices that occur in your head, body, and life—your thoughts, feelings, physical sensations, memories, and roles. To be an effective anthropologist, you must use observational methods that allow you to gain valuable information without intruding on or impacting that which is being studied. You use an etic, or science-oriented, approach that allows you to observe separately and impartially. As the anthropologist, you don't become one with these experiences; rather, you must remain a separate observer of them.

Summary

Self-as-context refers to a sense of self that transcends the content of internal experiences. It's the notion that we are not our thoughts, feelings, sensations, memories, stories, and roles; rather, we are the vessel that contains them. We contact this sense of self most readily via the observer perspective: being aware of awareness, or noticing that we're noticing. From this stance, we can safely contact uncomfortable or unwanted internal experiences in a nonthreatening way. This gives us the freedom and flexibility to move toward valued actions.

◆   ◆   ◆

Metaphors and Exercises Targeting Self-as-Context and Perspective Taking

Metaphors and Exercises in This Chapter

- Talking and Listening
- Observing Self with Values
- Fusion with Self-Evaluations
- I Can't Possibly _____
- Conceptualized Self on Trial
- The Classroom
- The Sky and the Weather
- The Prince and the Beggar
- Taking Off Your Armor
- Muntu
- The Anthropologist

In addition, the following exercises and metaphors, available in the sources cited, also target self-as-context and perspective taking.

Other Exercises

- Experientially, I'm Not That (Hayes, 2005, pp. 97–98)
- Label Parade (Walser & Westrup, 2007, pp. 126–131)
- Letting Go of Identity (Walser & Westrup, 2007, pp. 136–137)
- Mental Polarity (Hayes et al., 1999, p. 190)

- Observer (Hayes et al., 1999, pp. 192–196)

- Pick an Identity…Any Identity (Hayes et al., 1999, pp. 196–197)

- Retelling Your Own Story (Hayes, 2005, pp. 91–92)

Another Metaphor

- Chessboard (Hayes et al., 1999, pp. 190–192, 219, 268)

CHAPTER 7

VALUES

Living a valued life is, in essence, what ACT is all about. In ACT, values are chosen paths that the individual defines as important and meaningful. Values are actions and qualities of actions and therefore are stated with verbs and adverbs, such as "give generously" or "connect lovingly." They aren't things we have, stated with nouns and adjectives, such as "an expensive car" or "a pretty face" (Hayes, 2005). Luoma and colleagues describe valuing eloquently: "We engage in an act of valuing each time we do something that is purposive or instrumental. We value various qualities of outcomes; we value ways of living; we value ideals; we value what kind of friend, lover, partner, parent, child, or worker we are. These implicit purposive qualities of any instrumental act are elevated to a value by the action of choosing that very quality" (2007, p. 131). A life driven by values is characterized by fullness, purpose, and vital engagement.

Values are personal. What is important to you may not be important to your spouse, and what is valued by a client's parents, religious group, or society may not be important to the client. To facilitate this distinction, you might ask, "If no one knew you were doing this, would it still be important to you?" Values are also enduring in the sense that they cannot be achieved or completed. For example, you never finish connecting lovingly with your children.

What Values Are Not

Some clients may have assumptions about what values are that can serve as barriers to working with values. Therefore, it's generally a good idea to begin this work by explaining how values are defined in ACT, clarifying both what values are and what they are not.

Values Are Not Internal States

When clients first start working to identify values, they often say things like "I value feeling calm" or "I value being pain-free." Of course, this is a trap because feelings can't be controlled. In fact, the pursuit of feeling calm or pain-free is often exactly what keeps clients stuck in an unworkable life (e.g., avoiding anything that creates anxiety or pain, even if those things are very important). If a client identifies a feeling state as a value, you can help her identify the true underlying value by asking something like "If you did feel calm (were pain-free, etc.), what might you be doing that you're not doing now? And what would you no longer do that you are doing now? Also, how would you like to be as you're doing or not doing those things?" This will return the focus to behavior and may also provide insight into some of the client's patterns of experiential avoidance.

If the client seems really stuck on this concept, insisting that she values something like "feeling at peace," you'll probably need to revisit previous ACT concepts, specifically control or struggle as the problem, creative hopelessness, and acceptance and willingness. The exercises throughout this book can facilitate an experiential review of these other core concepts, and we believe this will provide a far more powerful understanding than a didactic explanation can. To help clients see values more broadly, you might share the appendix D with them; it offers a lengthy list of words people often use to describe values.

Values Are Not About How People Treat Us

Clients may state values along the lines of a desire to be loved, to get respect, or to be included as part of a group. However, these kinds of things are controlled by others, whereas values are about how the individual chooses to behave. So while there may be actions a client can take to increase the likelihood of being loved, respected, or included, those outcomes can't be guaranteed. Clients' chosen values should reflect what they truly want to stand for, such as acting in ways that are compassionate, honest, or assertive—whatever is consistent with who the client really wants to be—rather than indicating what the client would like to receive from others. If the outcome of a valued action that involves others doesn't fulfill the wishes that coexist with the value, the ACT therapist will validate any painful feelings that arise and encourage acceptance and continued engagement with values nonetheless.

Values Are Not Goals

Goals, by definition, can be completed or achieved. They can be checked off a to-do list. Some examples of goals might be getting a master's degree in social work, buying flowers for a romantic partner, or reading a light novel. When used as a means for traveling a valued path, goals can be quite constructive. If a client values helping others, being a loving partner, or indulging in recreation, then the goals above can work in the service of keeping the client heading in the direction of her values.

The danger of goals, however, is that once they are achieved, movement down the valued path may halt. To live a valued life, clients must remain consistently engaged with their values and commit to ongoing valued actions. For example, Jose gives his wife flowers (accomplishing a goal) in the service of being a loving spouse (a value). Just because he achieved this goal doesn't mean he's finished being a loving spouse. Because being a loving spouse is one of Jose's values, by definition it can never be completed. Jose must find ways to walk the path of a loving spouse in a consistent, ongoing way. One day he might give his wife flowers. The next day he might commit to communicating with her in a mindful, loving way.

The Function of Values in ACT

The language of the mind often pulls people away from a meaningful life by presenting mental obstacles, or thoughts. When we believe these thoughts, we become mired in cognitive fusion and experiential avoidance. This inevitably creates distance between us and our values. People tend to put off valued living until their thoughts and feelings can be "fixed." For example, someone might wait to start dating until he loses weight, even though intimate relationships are very important to him. Or someone might wait to give a professional presentation until she feels more like an expert, even though professional growth is very important to her.

ACT isn't about fixing or changing internal private events; it's about changing behaviors. Values provide the road map for making these changes. They define the type of person we want to be, the way we want to live, who we are, and what we want to stand for. Values inspire everything we do in ACT. Acceptance and willingness, defusion, present-moment awareness, and self-as-context are all practiced in the service of promoting greater flexibility for living in accordance with personal values. Putting values into action, or walking the walk, known as committed action, will be the topic of the next chapter.

Values Exercises

A number of experiential exercises have been developed to help clients identify and clarify their values. In this section we offer several that we find particularly helpful.

◆　◆　◆

THE PRIME-TIME NEWS STORY
(Stephen Sheets & Jill Stoddard, 2013)

The Prime-Time News Story is an eyes-closed exercise done in two parts. The first part aims at identifying the ways in which clients are currently living their life. The second part aims at identifying the ways in which they'd ideally like to be living. Highlighting the discrepancies between the two will give you fodder for values work. As with any eyes-closed exercise, you can begin by having clients focus on their breath or how they're sitting to help them get present before moving on to the visualization. In this example, we use news anchor Brian Williams, but feel free to substitute any other well-known newscaster or a television personality who interviews celebrities.

> *I'd like you to start by closing your eyes and doing your best to just follow my voice and imagine the following scenario as vividly as you can: Imagine Brian Williams is doing a biographical story on your life up to today. The story will include a highlight reel with all of the important people and events in your life, as well as an interview with you. The highlight reel will depict the type of person you've been, what you've stood for, the roles you've played, and your purpose. This will be a story commemorating the life you've lived up to today.*
>
> *Imagine how this story would go. When Brian Williams interviews you, what would you tell him about the type of person you've been, the type of life you've led, and the choices you've made? What would you say to him about the roles you've played? What type of spouse, parent, friend, child, sibling, worker, student, or supervisor have you been?* (List roles that are relevant to the client.) *What might you say about the ways you've handled pain, anxiety, or depression and the limits these have placed on you?* (Again, use examples that are relevant to the client.) *What would you say about the things that are most important to you?*
>
> *Take the next few moments to picture the highlight reel of your life and the background narration that would accompany it.... When you're ready, come back to the room, open your eyes, and tell me what you said, heard, and saw.*

Write down anything the client shares, validating the experience and especially highlighting points of struggle or experiential avoidance and lack of clarity regarding his values. Then move on to the second part of the exercise.

Now I'd like you to close your eyes again. This time I'd like you to imagine that we've fast-forwarded many years into the future, and Brian Williams's protégé is doing a follow-up story on your life. This story starts where the previous one left off, and it's a depiction of the ways you lived your life in complete accordance with the things that were most important to you. Once again, imagine the highlight reel and narration for this story. What would be said about your values, the type of person you were, the type of life you led, and the choices you made? What would now be said about the roles you played? What might be said about the ways you handled pain, anxiety, and depression? What might be said about how you approached the things that were most important to you?

Spend the next few moments imagining the follow-up story and noticing any differences between the story of your life up to today and the story of your life from this point forward. When you're ready, come back to the room, open your eyes, and tell me what you heard and saw.

Give the client enough time to think about this, then engage in a discussion, writing down anything important the client shares. Use the information to start fleshing out the client's personal values, highlighting the discrepancies between where he is and where he wants to be.

◆　◆　◆

MIND-READING MACHINE
(Harris, 2009, p. 201)

The Mind-Reading Machine is a quick and simple exercise to get clients thinking about personal values by imagining themselves from the perspective of someone close to them.

Imagine that I have a mind-reading machine that's tuned into the mind of someone very important to you, so that you can hear that person's every thought. As you tune in, that person is thinking about you: about what you stand for, what your strengths are, what you mean to him or her, and the role you play in his or her life. In an ideal world, where you've lived your life as the person you truly want to be, what would you hear this person thinking?

♦ ♦ ♦

THE HEROES

(Rob Archer, 2013)

The Heroes exercise is a great way to help clients identify personal qualities that are important to them as a way to start a conversation about values.

> *Think about your heroes. Consider people who have played a direct role in your life: family members, friends, teachers, coaches, teammates, and so on. Now think about people who have inspired you indirectly: authors, artists, celebrities, or even fictional characters. Who would you most like to be like? Pick one person you really admire.* (Give the client time to think about this.) *Now think about all the qualities you really admire in this person—not the person's circumstances, but personal qualities—and write them down. Once you've done this, I'd like you to look this over and think about how these might translate into your own personal values.*

Discuss the specific qualities that come up. Clients might write things like "ambitious," "selfless," "generous," "thoughtful," "kind," "compassionate," "creative," and so on. Ask clients how they think they are like this person or unlike this person, and in what ways they might like to move toward being more like this person. Help them identify the life domains (friendships, family, career, and so on) in which they might be willing to work on building these qualities. This can lead to a discussion of obstacles and how clients might use other ACT processes, such as acceptance, present-moment awareness, defusion, and self-as-context, to handle those obstacles in the service of moving forward in a values-consistent way. In appendix E, you'll find a worksheet to use with this exercise. You can also create your own worksheet.

♦ ♦ ♦

THE SWEET SPOT

(Wilson & DuFrene, 2009, p. 203–209)

The Sweet Spot is a great exercise to use early in values work because it transcends the evaluations that often come along with simply asking clients what matters to them. It can also create a powerful connection between therapist and client, especially when done as a mindfulness exercise or when the therapist shares a sweet moment of his or her own. Two scripts are provided below: the first for an eyes-open discussion, and the second for an eyes-closed mindfulness exercise. Both versions are aimed at generating an initial discussion about identifying values.

DISCUSSION SCRIPT

We've talked a lot about your symptoms, problems, and difficult thoughts and feelings, as well as some of the things you do to try to avoid those thoughts and feelings. I think I'm starting to understand this pain and struggle. But what I'd like to talk about today is really different from that. I want to try to understand a moment in your life where you experienced sweetness—an experience you had where maybe you let go of the struggle with your thoughts and feelings, even if just for a little while. It doesn't have to be the biggest or most monumental thing that's happened—or it could be. Just pick any moment, big or small, recent or long ago, when you felt really present, engaged, or alive.

You might find yourself engaging in a little mental ping-pong right now, trying to choose the "right" or "best" moment. See if you can notice that and let go of that struggle, just settling onto whatever sweet spot shows up. (You might choose to share your own example here; if you do, be sure to really settle into it as you share, letting yourself fully experience each detail as you describe it.) *Let me know when you have one.*

Okay, now I want you to take a minute to really notice all the details that were present in that moment, using the senses in your mind's eye. What did you see and how did it appear? Was anyone with you? How did any others appear? What kinds of sounds, smells, or tastes were there? How were you feeling? Once you have the whole image, I'd like you to share the details of your sweet moment with me in a way that helps me get that this was a moment where you felt true sweetness.

Sometimes clients may rush through this as if they're giving the facts of a police report. Your job is to be present and notice where clients get hung up in too much explaining and not enough expressing. Slow them down and ask them to linger on details. You want them to revisit this experience and really connect to the sweetness again—and to connect with you as you appreciate their moment of sweetness. This may occur more powerfully when the Sweet Spot is done as an eyes-closed mindfulness exercise, described below.

Once clients have shared their sweet moment, reflect back the things you noticed that might be important to them based on the moment of sweetness they shared. For example, one client shared her experience of finishing a race she ran with good friends.

Themes of accomplishment, physical health, togetherness, and shared experiences arose in our discussion.

The experiences clients share can also provide an opportunity to notice moments of acceptance, defusion, or committed action, especially in regard to things they don't share. For instance, in the example of the client who finished a race with good friends, the therapist might point out some of the difficult or painful things the client must have endured to get to the point of finishing the race: muscle aches, injuries, finding time in a busy schedule to train, running in bad weather, doubts about her ability to finish, anxiety about finding the race site and being on time, and so on. In this case, the therapist might say, "I can't help but notice that this whole process wasn't easy, and yet those details didn't really show up in your narrative. It seems to me that honoring your body and sharing this accomplishment with your friends was important enough that you were willing to endure and accept some of these challenges. And it seems that despite these challenges, or maybe in part because of them, you were still able to find sweetness in those moments. I wonder how this might apply to some other areas of your life?"

MINDFULNESS SCRIPT

In a moment I'm going to ask you to close your eyes as I lead you in an exercise where you'll bring your attention to a sweet spot in your life. It can be very simple. Let me give you an example.

You should share your own example, really settling into the details as they are expressed. Here's an example showing how a therapist could use her own experience to help the client come up with a sweet spot.

I was sitting in the rocker in my baby girl's nursery, with her warm little eight-month-old body snuggled up on my lap. She had that fresh-out-of-the-tub baby smell, and she was resting her little body against mine while I read her a bedtime story and we rocked. Then, all of a sudden, my husband peeked his face around the corner of her bedroom door and said "Boo!" She squealed and wiggled, and I just sat there watching the two loves of my life playing a delightfully silly game of peekaboo. In that moment, I thought, This is my family. It was a two-minute moment that was completely perfect and sweet.

So I'll ask you to think about some sweet spot of your own. It doesn't have to be like mine. And again, it can be something very simple. But do think about something specific. It could be taking a first sip of coffee on a Sunday morning when you're settling down with the paper. It could be watching a sunset or paddling a kayak—anything whatsoever. Sometimes when you're watching your kids as they play, there are times when they don't see you watching them and you really see them. Maybe that's your sweet spot. Whatever it is, I'd like to invite you to encounter that sweet moment. Afterward, I'm going to ask you to open your eyes and express this sweet moment—just give voice to it.

You're likely to run into a problem in that you'll want to explain yourself. Maybe you'll think, I'm not really explaining myself so that she really gets how sweet this was for me. You'll want to solve that problem. If you find yourself doing that, you have the same job you would have if, for example, you noticed yourself making a grocery list while doing sitting meditation. Your job is to notice that and then gently come back to your breath. Just give voice to this sweet moment, letting it pour from you, as if you took a glass of water and let that water pour out. If there's any effort involved, just notice that and let yourself go silent. Then come back to giving expression to your sweet moment.

My job will be to appreciate your moment of sweetness as you share it. I may not totally understand, but I will appreciate it in much the same way I might experience a sunset. There's no need to evaluate it or understand the science of light refraction. The experience can simply be appreciated.

Now allow yourself to sit comfortably and gently let your eyes close. I'd like you to begin by noticing the different sounds in the room. Imagine that you have a sort of checklist. Begin with the most prominent sounds, and as you notice them, imagine checking them off the list. Then see if you can listen for softer, more subtle sounds. And breathe.

Begin to draw your attention to your body. Slowly begin to notice the place where you body makes contact with the floor, with the chair. And breathe. Notice in particular the little places where you can feel the transition in that contact, the very edges of the place on your back that's touching the chair. See if, in your mind's eye, you can trace that very edge. See if you can begin to notice the small details in sensation that tell you one part is touching and the next is not. And breathe.

Now imagine that in front of you is a file cabinet. Imagine that you can open the drawer, reach in, and withdraw a picture—a picture of you during that sweet moment. Let yourself take that picture out of the file cabinet. Feel it in your hands. Let yourself look into that face of yours in the picture. Notice the look on your face in that picture and the details surrounding you.

Now imagine that your awareness is some sort of liquid that you can pour into the you in that picture. Imagine that you're beginning to pour your awareness into the skin of that you in that picture at that very moment. See if you can let yourself emerge in that place at that particular moment. Imagine opening your eyes in that place and let yourself see what you see there. Let yourself notice the sensations that you feel on your skin in that place. If you're outdoors, perhaps you feel a slight breeze. If you're with someone, you might feel the warmth of that person's skin against you or the scent of that person's hair. Let it be as if you can just breathe that moment in, as if each breath fills you with that sweetness. Let it be as if every cell in your body can feel what it is to be in that moment. Take a moment to luxuriate in that experience and let the sweetness fill you up slowly like some kind of liquid. (Give the client a few moments of silence to do this.)

Now I'm going to ask you to gently let your eyes open. When you're ready, begin to speak and give expression to that moment, letting me really hear, feel, and see that sweet moment, and staying with it.

Debrief the exercise by thanking clients for sharing their experience and asking how it was for them. You can bring in elements of various ACT core processes as suggested above. You might also discuss the impact the exercise had on the sense of connection between the client and you.

♦ ♦ ♦

WRITING YOUR AUTOBIOGRAPHY
(Mark J. Stern, 2013)

Like the exercise Prime-Time News Story, Writing Your Autobiography is an eyes-closed exercise done in two parts. The first part aims at identifying ways in which the client imagines she would like to ideally live her life. The second part looks at ways in which she's currently living. Highlighting the discrepancies between the two provides a direction for values work.

Whenever you read an autobiography, you get a sense for who the person was, how the person lived, and what he or she stood for. Themes of values and priorities show up throughout an autobiography. I'd like to do an exercise where you imagine your own autobiography.

I want you to close your eyes, take a deep breath, and imagine that you've lived a long and fulfilling life—a life full of meaning. Imagine that you've been the person you wanted to be and stood for what was important to you. And now you're writing your story as an autobiography. What would you want to express about yourself? What would you want your readers to learn about you?

Right now, I want you to focus on the overall image of how you lived and who you became, rather than the details of how you got there. (If a client isn't quite sure what you mean, you can give an example, but don't give too many; you want this to be the client's innovation.) *For example, if people read that you spent the last thirty years making considerable efforts to eat right, go to the gym regularly, or manage an illness well, they might get the impression that you were someone who valued your health. What other values would you feel proud to have emerge when you write your autobiography?*

Ask the client to list a number of values, including behaviors that would reflect those values. You can work on this together with the client in session or assign it as homework. If you assign it as homework, you can give the client the handout in appendix F.

Now I want you to close your eyes again. Begin to imagine your autobiography as it might unfold if you were to write it today. What messages or values would be highlighted in your present-day story? What would you write about the person you are, the choices you make, and how you live your life?

Again, you can either work on this together with the client in session or assign it as homework, using the worksheet provided in appendix F.

Then, after completing both autobiographies, either together in session or as homework, process the exercise with the client, highlighting discrepancies between the person the client would like to be and the person she currently is. This can lead to a discussion of committed actions, obstacles to those actions, and how ACT strategies, including the exercises and metaphors in this book, can be used to overcome those obstacles in the service of moving forward with valued actions.

◆   ◆   ◆

TEN STEPS TO TRYING ON A VALUE
(Dahl, Plumb, Stewart, & Lundgren, 2009, pp. 164–165)

The exercise Ten Steps to Trying On a Value is helpful for clients who don't have a strong sense of their values. Rather than needing to decide which values are important before choosing how to act, clients can experiment with different values, behaving consistently with them for a while. This allows them to learn from direct experience how it feels to commit to behaving consistently with a freely chosen value and, over time, can help them discover which values may have personal meaning for them.

Working with clients around this issue, targeting willingness, defusion, or letting go of needing to choose the "correct" value right away, will be helpful. It's best to assign this as homework for an extended period of time, at least a week or two, and longer if possible. This will help clients build a longer history of behaving consistently with a value before coming to a decision about whether to continue moving forward in the direction of that value or choosing another value. Here are the steps, along with suggested scripts for describing each step.

1. **Choose a value.** *Choose a valued direction that you're willing to try on for at least a week. This should be a value that you can enact and that you care about. This isn't a time to try to change others or manipulate them into changing.*

2. **Notice reactions.** *Notice anything that comes up about whether or not this is a "good" value, or whether you really care about this value. Just notice all thoughts for what they are. Remember that your mind's job is to create thoughts. Let your mind do that while you continue with the exercise.*

3. **Make a list.** *Take a moment to list a few behaviors that are related to the chosen value.*

4. **Choose a behavior.** *From this list, choose a behavior or set of behaviors that you can commit to doing between now and the next session or the next few sessions.*

5. **Notice judgments.** *Notice anything that comes up about whether or not that's a good behavior, whether you'll enjoy it, or whether you can actually do the action you're committing to.*

6. **Make a plan.** *Write down how you'll go about enacting this value in the very near future (today, tomorrow, this weekend, and so on). Consider anything you'll need to plan or get in order, such as calling someone, cleaning the house, or making an appointment. Choose when to do that—the sooner, the better.*

7. **Just behave.** *Even if this value involves other people, don't tell them what you're doing. See what you can notice if you just enact this value without telling others about the experiment you're doing.*

8. **Commit.** *Commit to following your plan every day. Notice anything that shows up as you do so.*

9. **Keep a daily diary of your reactions.** *Things to look for and record in your diary include other people's reactions to you; any thoughts, feelings, or bodily sensations that occur before, during, or after the behavior; and how you feel doing your chosen action for the second (or fifth, or tenth, or hundredth) time. Watch for evaluations that indicate whether this activity, value, or valued direction was "good" or "bad" or judgments about others or yourself in relation to living this value. Gently thank your mind for those thoughts and see if you can choose not to buy into the judgments your mind makes about the activity.*

10. **Reflect.** *Bring your diary to your next therapy session so we can discuss your experience and make a plan for moving forward.*

◆　◆　◆

TABLE OF VALUES
(Jill Stoddard, 2013)

The Table of Values is inspired by the Goals, Actions, Barriers Form (Hayes et al., 1999, p. 227), in this case designed to be used by clients, rather than the therapist. It also has additional columns for core ACT processes that might be helpful and specific exercises that can help manage obstacles in the service of moving forward with valued actions. Collaboratively completing the Values and Committed Action Worksheet with clients can be a helpful way to make some of these concepts concrete for them. A blank form is provided in appendix G; an example will follow.

Area of importance	Parenting	Romantic relationships
How I want to be	1. A good listener 2. Setting limits when necessary 3. Loving, comforting, compassionate	1. Open to meeting someone new 2. Open, vulnerable, genuine
Things I can do	1. Set aside time to ask my kids how their day was. 2. Give praise for good behavior and consequences for bad. 3. Give hugs.	1. Go on a date. 2. Share personal information about myself.
What might get in my way	1. Frustration, impatience 2. Wanting my kids to like me 3. Exhaustion	1. Fear of rejection 2. What if I tell him things and he thinks I'm stupid or boring or doesn't like me?
How I can move forward	Acceptance, defusion, mindfulness	Defusion
Exercises	Boat on the Water	Floating Leaves on a Moving Stream; Pickle, Pickle, Pickle

◆ ◆ ◆

PERSONAL JOB AD
(Rob Archer, 2013)

The following exercise was inspired by Roman Krznaric's writings on finding work (2012), where it was written specifically to help people struggling with career decisions, and further modified by Rob Archer (2013) for use in practice. However, you could adapt this exercise for someone who's looking for a romantic partner, considering moving to a new city, and so on.

We're used to looking at and replying to job ads. The trick is to try to match the job description as much as we can.

What if organizations had to apply to you? Imagine that there's a new jobs section in the newspaper want ads, and instead of having organizations advertising specific jobs, it contains information about people offering themselves, and employers apply if they can provide a role that meets the candidate's requirements. Write your personal job ad, advertising to the world the kind of person you are and what you care about, but don't specify a particular job or profession. Make sure that your ad includes the following:

Your name and maybe a personal motto

Personal qualities, such as generous, impatient, or introverted

Talents or skills, such as playing the trombone or designing spreadsheets

Values, such as wanting to make a difference

Ambitions, such as "I want to run my own business" or "I want to be paid well enough to take a vacation twice a year"

Anything else you wish for in your ideal job, such as "I want a job where I am an expert (laugh a lot, can use my Spanish, can travel, and so on)"

Jobs that need not apply, such as "I don't want a job that requires travel"

One thing you cannot compromise on, such as "I won't take a job where I can't be outdoors"

Here's an example:

Name and motto: *Bob Bowman. The best in me brings out the best in others.*

Personal qualities: *Open, curious, generous, compassionate, anxious, ambitious, courageous, bright, determined*

Talents: *Social intelligence, psychology and counseling, sports, creativity*

Values: *Meaning, freedom, status, courage, integrity*

Ambitions: *I want to build something. I want to make a difference to other people. I want to build a movement that changes the way people see work. I want to use psychology to help people cope with their suffering.*

Anything else you wish for in your ideal job: *I want to be an expert in something and to pass this expertise on. I want to build effective tools that help people move forward and to make these accessible for free. I want to be very well paid, but want this to reflect my value to others. I want to write brilliant books that aren't afraid to challenge convention. I want to travel a bit. I want to live in the United States one day. I want to have a family and dedicate time to them. I want to work with brilliant, like-minded people.*

Jobs that need not apply: *Anything to do with bureaucracy. Selling things that people don't need. Anything that has no evidence to support it. Anything that relies on drinking.*

One thing you cannot compromise on: *My values.*

Values Metaphors

Several metaphors can be used to illustrate values and related concepts. This section provides several that we find helpful for various issues that arise around values, such as the differences between values and goals, prioritizing or balancing values, and making choices or changes that are driven by values. Also note that many other values metaphors are widely available on the Internet, such as the Magical Bank Account and the Humble Fisherman (sources unknown), should you wish to broaden your choices even further.

◆ ◆ ◆

THE SCOREBOARD

(Taryn Gammon & Jill Stoddard, 2013)

The Scoreboard is a metaphor designed to demonstrate the difference between values and goals. It also illustrates the ways in which values should help identify goals, underscoring the futility of goals in a valueless vacuum. You can tailor it to specific clients by using different sports or even changing the sport to a board game. For this example, we'll use football.

What's your favorite sport to play?... Okay, imagine playing football. It's a crisp fall day and the players are lined up on offense and defense. The quarterback gives the signal for the center to hike the ball, then drops back for the pass and throws to the receiver, who breaks a tackle and runs into the end zone for a touchdown. And so it goes for the next couple of hours, up and down the field—first downs, field goals, tackles, touchdowns. The other team scores, your team catches up. The other team pulls ahead again, but in the last nail-biting seconds of the game, your team pulls out a big play for the win! The final score on the scoreboard reads 21 for your team, and 14 for the opposing team.

Now what if the scorekeeper were to come along at the beginning of the game and offer to put that score up on the board for you? Your team gets 21 points, the other team gets 14, so you win—game over; no need to play for it. Would you take him up on it? (Clients always say no.) *Why not?* (Give clients an opportunity to answer.)

This is like the difference between values and goals. Winning the game might be your goal, and you may or may not accomplish it. But what's truly important is the process by which you achieve that goal. It's really more about how you play the game. That's like the value.

Take some time to discuss the metaphor with the client. Clients often get overly focused on goals, and in ACT we want the focus to be more on values and actions that can be taken in the service of values. If clients wish to set goals as part of that framework, that's perfectly fine, but the goal should always be couched in the value.

Another issue that arises with goals is that, if they aren't achieved, clients sometimes stop engaging in other actions in service of the underlying value. In such cases, you can return to the Scoreboard metaphor and ask, "If you hadn't won the game, would it still be important to you to keep playing?" You can discuss building patterns of committed action even when specific goals aren't met, using exercises and metaphors from chapter 8 to facilitate committed action.

◆ ◆ ◆

REMODELING THE HOUSE

(Mark J. Stern, 2013)

Remodeling the House is a metaphor for making life changes or choices that are dictated by values. The foundation of the house symbolizes values, and the appliances, paint, and other accoutrements symbolize goals and actions.

> *Imagine remodeling your home. You're excited to choose attractive new tiles and modern appliances and to paint the walls in cool new colors. Your budget is set, and you have everything all planned out. But then you find out that there's a major crack in your foundation. Trying to figure out how to live your life (how to solve this problem, how to make this choice, and so on) before you decide who you really want to be and what you want to stand for would be like going forward with your remodel without fixing the foundation.*
>
> *If you hang pretty drapes and lay cozy carpets but your foundation is broken, your house will ultimately start to lean or cave in. You need to spend some extra time and money now to repair the foundation properly, and this may mean you can't immediately afford the attractive tile and modern appliances. However, at the end of the day you'll have a solid home. Identifying your values is like creating a solid foundation for your home. Living in alignment with your values doesn't guarantee that everything you want will occur or that you'll necessarily feel comfortable. But you will know that you're on the right track, and you'll be living a fuller, richer, more meaningful life that's congruent with the person you want to be. Living a valued life means that even when things don't go perfectly, not only will you still be standing, you'll maintain the integrity of the building.*

◆ ◆ ◆

THE CLASSROOM PROFESSOR

(Jill Stoddard, 2013)

The Classroom Professor is a well-known metaphor that can be found all over the Internet under a variety of names. Although its original source is a mystery, it has appeared in print in several books (e.g., Addleman, 2004). It's a great metaphor for addressing the prioritization of values and balancing the things we have to do with what's really important to us. It can also be used to discuss competing values.

A professor stood before his college class with a large empty jar on the table in front of him. He filled the empty jar with ping-pong balls and asked the students if the jar was full. They agreed that it was.

Then the professor picked up a container of small rocks and poured them into the jar so they filled the spaces between the ping-pong balls. Again, he asked the students if the jar was full. They agreed it was.

Next, the professor picked up a bag of sand and poured it into the jar, filling the spaces between the small stones. He asked once more if the jar was full. The students responded with a unanimous yes.

The professor then produced two beers from under the table and poured these into the jar, filling the spaces between the grains of sand.

The professor then said, "This jar represents your life. The ping-pong balls are the important things—your family, your kids, your physical health, your friendships, and your passions—things that if everything else was lost and only they remained, your life would still be full. The small rocks are the other things that matter, like your career, your home, and your car. The sand is everything else—the little stuff. If you put the sand in the jar first," he continued, "you won't be able to fit all of the little rocks, let alone the ping-pong balls. The same goes for life. If you spend all of your time and energy on the little stuff, you won't have space for the things that are most vital to you. Make time for the things that are crucial to a meaningful life. Play with your kids. Take time to see your doctor. Go on a date with your spouse or partner. Go on vacation. There will always be time to do the chores and change the lightbulbs. Prioritize the ping-pong balls first, the things that really matter. The rest is just sand."

One of the students raised her hand and asked about the two beers. The professor smiled. "I'm glad you asked. It just goes to show you that no matter how full your life may seem, there's always room for a couple of beers with a friend."

Use this as an opportunity to discuss balance. Many of the things at the sand level need to be done, but perhaps not as frequently or extensively as the client is doing them. A client may do things at the sand level out of avoidance (e.g., cleaning her house to escape feelings of anxiety), and this may come at the expense of the ping-pong balls (e.g., excessive housecleaning leaves less time to play with her daughter). In appendix H, you'll find a worksheet you can use with this metaphor. You can also create your own.

♦   ♦   ♦

THE AEROSPACE ENGINEER

(Erik Andrews and Jill Stoddard, 2013)

Sometimes when clients start to pursue valued directions, they put all their energy into one area at the expense of another. The Aerospace Engineer is a great metaphor for discussing the importance of balance in identifying and pursuing values. It also allows for discussion about fusion pulling clients away from valued living.

> *Imagine that you're an aerospace engineer and you're sitting at a control panel watching an aircraft flight on a screen in front of you. Your job is to adjust the dials that control the weight, lift, drag, and thrust of the aircraft in order to keep it flying effectively. All of these elements are equally important, and if you don't make the needed adjustments, or if you overcorrect, the plane won't be able to fly effectively. You have to find the right balance for the smoothest flight.*
>
> *Now, although you have control over these adjustments, other factors remain out of your control. For example, you didn't design or build the aircraft. You can't control the weather. If the engine fails, this isn't your fault. But if you get hooked by worries about the factors that are out of your control, it may impact your adjustment of the weight, lift, drag, and thrust, and this may negatively impact your flight. The important thing here is to focus on the factors you can control and keep them in balance for the smoothest flight. If the weather happens to get rough or an engine does fail, your job is to do what you need to do to keep the plane in the air.*

Spend a few minutes talking about the metaphor and asking the client how he interprets it. He should see that the job of the engineer—identifying and adjusting factors that are within his control (i.e., weight, lift, drag, and thrust)—symbolizes the importance of balancing a variety of values. Making adjustments and keeping the aircraft flying, despite factors such as bad weather or engine trouble, symbolize committed action. Worries about the design of the plane and the weather symbolize fusion with internal experiences that can create obstacles to moving forward with values.

♦ ♦ ♦

THE CYCLING RACE
(Philippe Vuille, 2013)

The Cycling Race is a great metaphor to help clients identify one primary value to focus on. You might use this metaphor early on in values work or if it seems a client might become overwhelmed by more complicated values exercises, such as those exploring numerous life domains. This metaphor also has the benefit of offering a nice cross between identifying a value and encouraging the next step: committed action.

In a way, life is like a cycling race. We are all pedaling, and we wear shirts with words written on them. In French there is a phrase—Vous roulez pour qui?—that translates literally into "For whom do you travel?" The idea is the same as the one Bob Dylan expresses in the song "You've Gotta Serve Somebody." We sometimes believe it's possible to have blank shirts without anything written on them or that we can not know what we're pedaling in the service of. But even then, we nevertheless do have something written on our shirts, namely "Nothing" or "I don't know what I'm pedaling for." How would it feel to know that you're traveling for that master?

Now imagine there's a shop with piles of shirts with all kinds of words written on them: "Elegance," "Generosity," "Loyalty," "Health," "Love," "Caring," Honesty," and so on. And you can choose, for free, any one of them. Which one would you choose?

And when you do choose, notice what happens. You may hear this voice that says, "Ha! 'Elegance,' are you kidding? Have you looked at yourself in a mirror? That one definitely isn't for you." Or maybe you'll hear a voice saying something like, "How come you want to take 'Caring,' with that crappy introverted personality of yours?" The question is, can you have all these thoughts and still take the shirt showing the quality you're choosing to make important in your life?

Now find a goal, preferably a small one—an action that would lead your life a tiny bit in the direction of that value. Then do it. Pedal that bike while wearing that shirt! Of course the voice will come with you—for the entire ride. See if you can welcome that voice without trying to make it quiet down, but also without obeying it.

Summary

Facilitating movement toward engagement in a life that's full and meaningful is what ACT is all about. One of the most critical steps in this process is values clarification. Values are qualities of behavior that reflect who we want to be and what we want to stand for. Fusion with thoughts (e.g., *I'm not a good enough therapist; I'll never really get this ACT stuff*) and unwillingness to experience uncomfortable feelings (e.g., anxiety, self-doubt, or self-consciousness) frequently lead to experiential avoidance (e.g., sticking with old, familiar, comfortable forms of therapy rather than trying new ACT metaphors or exercises). This pulls us away from values that are important to us (e.g., being an effective, cutting-edge therapist). ACT's core processes of acceptance, defusion, present-moment awareness, and self-as-context help all of us—clients and therapists alike—handle the internal experiences that pose obstacles to moving forward with values-based actions.

◆　◆　◆

Metaphors and Exercises Targeting Values

Metaphors and Exercises in This Chapter

- The Prime-Time News Story

- Mind-Reading Machine

- The Heroes

- The Sweet Spot

- Writing Your Autobiography

- Ten Steps to Trying On a Value

- Table of Values

- Personal Job Ad

- The Scoreboard

- Remodeling the House

- The Classroom Professor

- The Aerospace Engineer

- The Cycling Race

In addition, the following exercises and metaphors, available in the sources cited, also target values.

Other Exercises

- Argyle Socks (Hayes et al., 1999, pp. 211–212)

- Assessment of Values, Goals, Actions, and Barriers (Hayes et al., 1999, pp. 222–223)

- Attending Your Own Funeral (Hayes, 2005, pp. 166–170)

- Revisiting Childhood Wishes (Zettle, 2007, pp. 120–121)

- What Do You Want Your Life to Stand For? (aka Eulogy or Tombstone; Hayes et al., 1999, pp. 215–218)

Other Metaphors

- Compass (Zettle, 2007, pp. 124–125)

- Gardening (Hayes et al., 1999, pp. 219–220, 228)

- The Magic Pill (Zettle, 2007, pp. 197–198)

- Path Up the Mountain (Hayes et al., 1999, pp. 221–222)

- Skiing (Hayes et al., 1999, pp. 220–221)

CHAPTER 8

COMMITTED ACTION

Committed action is active and purposeful engagement in overt behavior that is in the service of moving in the direction of one's values. If heading west is the identified value and the mileposts mark goals along the way, committed action is the process of putting one foot in front of the other with willingness and the awareness that steep hills and scary river crossings will inevitably be present. When working on committed action, the role of the therapist is to help clients identify areas for behavior change that are linked with values-consistent goals, to support clients in taking effective action, and to promote the development of larger and larger patterns of effective, values-based action. In an approach similar to that of other forms of behavior therapy, in ACT committed action is fostered through goal setting, skills acquisition, exposure, behavioral activation, and the like. The focus may be on either increasing or decreasing a particular behavior. The work typically involves behavior-change efforts at several levels, linked to short-term, medium-term, and long-term behavioral goals.

Distinctions Between Committed Action in ACT and Other Therapies

In contrast to other behavior therapies, in ACT attaining goals is just one of the intended purposes of committed action. Establishing a behavioral goal and outlining the steps to move toward that goal is the context in which clients can experience full and flexible commitment to the process of engaging in values-based behavior. The behavior of flexibly committing to an action and then undertaking that action is just as important as achieving a particular outcome.

Further, the emphasis on process over outcome provides an opportunity to practice both behavioral and psychological flexibility. Let's look at an example: For a particular client, doing things with his partner is a goal in the service of his value of building intimacy in the relationship. Arranging a date night is an action that supports that goal. However, despite making his best effort to arrange a date night, the client doesn't have direct control over the outcome. The babysitter may call in sick, or the client's partner may be held up at work. Here's where a commitment to the process of values-based action rather than the achievement of a specific goal opens up the possibility of behaving flexibly. The client can hold on to the goal of doing things together with his partner even if date nights typically aren't successful. He can try other means of moving toward that goal, such as making sure to spend a few minutes of private time together after the kids go to bed. By being flexible, he can move toward the goal via a new avenue, much like water does when its flow is obstructed. Further, as he continues moving forward with committed actions, the client may come in contact with any number of emotional experiences he typically evaluates as negative, such as worry, disappointment, or rejection. The commitment to action necessitates willingness to experience these and other private events, providing an opportunity to build psychological flexibility.

Goals and Action Plans

After helping clients clarify their values and identifying specific areas where inaction or misguided actions may reflect experiential avoidance, it's important to help clients come up with specific, measurable, and practical values-based goals that are within their abilities. The process of developing workable goals and action plans is done collaboratively. Help clients remain alert to the pitfalls of setting vague goals, goals that are beyond their abilities (perhaps because they don't have a needed skill), or goals that function to move them away from an aversive experience rather than toward a chosen value (e.g., arguing less rather than being more supportive of a loved one). The initial work can focus on one or two valued domains, starting with short-term goals and small behavioral steps linked to those goals and the values that inform them. It can be effective to ask clients to commit to concrete and manageable values-based action plans early in the course of therapy. Experience with these bold moves will help clients build patterns of committed action that involve contact with difficult thoughts and feelings.

One issue that often arises when identifying goals and action plans is seemingly competing values. For example, a client may identify self-care and being a loving parent as key values. However, in the process of choosing goals and related action, she may pit one value against the other. For example, she may state that if she were to take a long, hot bath one evening a week in the service of self-care, she wouldn't be able to spend that time with her kids in the service of being a loving parent. In such cases, help clients recognize that they can aspire to travel in many broad life directions, and that these directions are not mutually exclusive. While there may be conflicts in goal-related activities (e.g., taking a bath and spending time with the kids can't occur at the same time), the values of self-care and being a loving parent are complementary aspirations. Any apparent conflict probably results from behavioral and psychological avoidance that stands in the way of choosing goals and actions flexibly.

Barriers to Committed Action

Barriers to committed action can take many forms. In addition to experiential barriers like difficult emotions, memories, and thoughts, clients also may face environmental barriers, such as poor social skills, lack of funds, or an unsupportive partner. It's important to differentiate between experiential and environmental barriers. The processes of acceptance, defusion, acceptance, present-moment awareness, and values are effective in overcoming experiential barriers. Environmental barriers, on the other hand, may require problem solving, psychoeducation, skill building, and other strategies that focus on shaping overt behavior.

Sometimes clients may say that certain barriers are environmental when they are actually being used for experiential avoidance. For example, consider a socially anxious client who doesn't complete a homework assignment of contacting a friend. She might say it wasn't possible to send an e-mail because her computer was broken. However, perhaps the client could have phoned her friend or used another means of communication, such as a text message. Therefore, it's likely that the true barrier to contacting her friend was experiential rather than environmental. Perhaps she was obstructed by difficult thoughts and emotions, such as fear of rejection or thoughts about her lack of worth as a friend. In such situations, helping clients identify their psychological reactions and become aware of the avoidance function behind seemingly external circumstances can promote behavioral flexibility.

People who seek therapy have typically neglected important areas in their lives. They can often recognize this avoidance or inaction, and that recognition may be what ultimately influenced them to seek therapy. You'll uncover many barriers to action in the course of ACT treatment. While experiential work on acceptance, defusion, and values can go a long way in building psychological flexibility, committed action is the realm where clients have abundant opportunities to develop a stance of acceptance and willingness toward experiential barriers to values-based action.

When working with clients to identify areas for committed action and supporting them in values-based, goal-directed behavior, many of the feared thoughts and feelings they were previously avoiding are bound to show up. Therefore, a review of potential experiential barriers that might lead them away from valued goals is likely to be beneficial in any discussion of homework assignments or committed actions to be taken in or out of session.

It's also essential for clients to monitor any psychological reactions that occur when they engage in committed actions or that prevent them from following through on committed actions. They may find it helpful to use goals and activities worksheets or a homework diary to keep track of specified goals, actions taken toward those goals, and barriers to committed action. (Appendix G offers a worksheet that can be useful here.) As noted above, contact with these potential obstacles can then be addressed with interventions that focus on acceptance, defusion, present-moment awareness, and values. Enhancing committed action is a necessarily iterative process that involves identifying goals, taking action, coming in contact with unpleasant and difficult psychological reactions, noting any pull toward experiential avoidance, and addressing the barriers.

Distinguishing Forms and Functions of Action

Uncovering the complexities that drive a client to behave in a certain way will help you distinguish behaviors that truly reflect valued living and those that serve some other purpose. Some behaviors that may look like values-based action in form may actually serve the function of experiential avoidance. This distinction between the form and the function of an action is especially important with clients who are seemingly living active and full lives when they come to therapy. Consider a client who identifies self-care as a value and goes to the gym every day after work as a move toward this value. Upon further exploration, you discover that he's having marital difficulties and doesn't want to face difficult conversations with his wife in the evenings. What appeared to be a committed action in the service of valued living is actually functioning as a way to avoid the discomfort associated with difficult private experiences that may arise when talking with his wife.

Another common issue that comes up is clients engaging in behavior related to certain values in excessive or inflexible ways. These actions often take the form of pleasing others or adhering to societal norms associated with values in domains such as family, friendship, community, or spirituality. For example, imagine a client who's extremely dedicated to her job and often works above and beyond her responsibilities. If she has identified having a strong work ethic as a value, on the surface this behavior may look like values-based action, with the choice to be hardworking seeming to echo her values-driven goal. But as you explore the issue further, the client reveals that she had a demanding father and felt she could never meet his expectations, no matter how hard she tried. You also learn that this client is persistently physically exhausted due to the long hours she puts in and work-related stress, and that she no longer has a sense of vitality or meaning in her work.

Discerning these issues as they come up is an important part of the therapeutic process and is guided by continued observation of client behavior through the lens of functional analysis. Learning what a client does excessively, or doesn't do enough of, in certain contexts, and why the client chooses to behave this way, will allow you to develop a better understanding of how a given behavior functions. Together, you and the client can work to discover what the client's behavior is in the service of, which will help guide the client's work on committed action and behavior change.

Building Larger Patterns of Action

The process of building committed action starts with small and manageable behaviors and gradually increases in scope and size to include larger patterns of action. It's important to keep in mind that committed action involves not just overt behavior in the service of chosen values, but also willingness to experience the thoughts, reactions, and emotional experiences that arise. As with learning any other skill, learning to undertake purposeful action with commitment and willingness is hard work and requires concentrated attention, time, and practice.

There are several benefits to starting small and gradually increasing to larger patterns of behavior over time (Luoma et al., 2007):

- Although willingness is an all-or-nothing stance, one can choose to be willing in one situation (e.g., reading advanced directive paperwork) and not another (e.g., making an appointment to complete and sign the advanced directive). Establishing small goals and modest action plans provides an opportunity to

155

practice small bouts of willingness in circumscribed situations. With practice and time, as willingness increases in relation to small goals, clients can be encouraged to take on larger goals or patterns of behavior.

- Starting with small goals and modest action plans heightens the likelihood of success, increasing the chances that clients will continue to engage in the process of setting and acting upon goals in the service of chosen values.

- Focusing clients' attention and intentions on the individual steps in larger patterns of action strengthens the link between behaviors and the values that govern those behaviors. This in turn strengthens the influence of values on behavior and undermines the power of the immediate consequences of behavior, as well as the power of the mind and its thoughts, evaluations, reasons, and so on.

Consider a young man whose long-term partner recently ended their relationship. As a result, he was experiencing a range of emotional, cognitive, and somatic experiences, including feelings of loneliness and sadness, negative self-image and self-esteem, and nausea and stomach pains. He also found himself spending long periods of time reflecting on memories associated with the relationship. In the context of a lost relationship, this man's experiences aren't out of the ordinary, but his willingness (or lack of willingness) to move forward in pursuing future relationships will have a significant impact on his ability to live a valued, meaningful life. In the course of therapy, this client recognized that although one of his values involved being in a loving relationship, he felt overwhelmed by how much time, effort, and emotional energy it would take to move in that direction. So part of the therapeutic work was to recognize that willingness to experience painful and difficult internal experiences was related to his values in regard to being in a loving relationship. The therapeutic approach also involved helping him understand that he need not be in a relationship in order to pursue that value. In fact, jumping into a relationship right after the breakup could function as experiential avoidance, filling the void his ex-partner had left. On the other hand, isolation and avoiding interaction with potential partners due to fears of being hurt again might also function as experiential avoidance.

For this young man, building larger patterns of willingness could eventually lead to more opportunities to engage with potential partners in a loving relationship. As a first step, he focused on healing in a way that was meaningful to him by taking time for himself and getting support from friends and family. After some time, he began to picture himself dating again, perhaps being set up through friends or trying online dating. As he started to contemplate reentering the world of dating and relationships, he experienced an increase in anxiety and insecurity. However, with an eye on his values, he continued to be open to dating and actually went out with several potential partners from different backgrounds. While dating brought with it all sorts of uncertainties, his willingness to experience this discomfort allowed him to learn about what characteristics best suited him in a long-term partner.

Exercises to Support Committed Action

Clients typically understand what it means to take action. However, they may not necessarily appreciate the unique qualities of committed action. Below are several exercises that can be used to support committed action.

◆ ◆ ◆

ZORG THE ALIEN

(Nuno Ferreira, 2013)

Zorg the Alien is an exercise that's usually presented after values clarification, preferably after clients have generated a list of values and potential valued actions. Its main function is to give clients a sense of where they are in valued living and where they want to be. The key aspect of this exercise is that it's done in a defused way using a behavior analytic approach.

> I'd like you to meet Zorg. He's an alien from a faraway galaxy who's traveling the universe to learn about other life-forms. In his travels, Zorg has met humans, and he knows that these amazing creatures who live on Earth have these things called values that guide the way they go through life. On this visit, Zorg has chosen you as his subject of study. He's up in space in his ship with a huge telescope focused on you, and he's just observing what you do.
>
> Let's suppose that Zorg has seen your list of values and valued actions. He knows what you value and how you'd behave if you were living according to those values. For the purposes of his study, and relying solely on observation of your behavior, Zorg has to score how much he thinks you're living according to your values. Remember, he can only see how you act, not how you wish to act.

Based on that, how do you think Zorg would score you in the life domains we've discussed? Let's say his scale goes from 0 to 10, with 0 meaning you aren't acting at all according to your values and 10 meaning that your actions are fully consistent with your values. What score do you think Zorg would give you? (Go through each valued domain individually and have the client assign a score to each one.)

Now think about the scores you'd like Zorg to give you. Let's go through all the domains again so you can say how you'd like to score in each.

After the scores are assigned, engage clients in a discussion about what's standing between where they are and where they want to be. Use other concepts, such as willingness and defusion, to explore how they can overcome these obstacles and facilitate moving in valued directions.

◆　◆　◆

THE BUBBLE

(Nuno Ferreira, 2013)

The Bubble is a combination of metaphor and exercise inspired by the Bubble metaphor presented in *Learning ACT* (Luoma et al., 2007, pp. 167–168). It's used after clients have experimented with committed actions, and allows them to contrast their experiences of life-expanding actions versus life-constricting ones. For this exercise, you need the graphics and worksheet provided in appendix I. The graphics illustrate the contrast between an expanding life and a constricted life, and the worksheet can help clients track the progression of therapy and the consequences of living a more mindful and accepting life in the service of personal values.

Over the past few weeks, you've probably seen yourself doing things that you weren't doing before. You took actions that you had been avoiding, taking them on because they have an important meaning for you. You've probably realized that by committing to those actions and following through on them, you've opened the door to more and more actions that will lead you in the directions you value. So you've started having more and more choices. The process of committed action is all about shifting from a life constricted by avoidance and fusion to a life where forward movement in the direction of your values and an expansion of your choices and actions are constant. When you're acting and moving in ways that are consistent with your values, you'll probably experience a sense of expansion in your life. Let's do an exercise to help you to get a feel for that.

Imagine that your life is a bubble made of a special material that can absorb everything around the bubble without ever breaking or bursting. You're the one controlling how much air is in the bubble, and therefore how much it expands or contracts. (Use the graphics in appendix I to demonstrate this.) Outside the bubble are these sharp objects; they are your difficult experiences. When you get scared about these sharp objects because they look like they're going to burst your bubble, you stop inflating it and your life contracts, as in the top graphic. When you accept these experiences into your life despite how sharp they look, willingly inflating your bubble so it comes in contact with these difficulties and absorbs them, your bubble expands, as in the bottom graphic.

Let's review the committed actions you undertook last week. Consider whether you did any of these actions in the service of your values and fully embracing everything you experienced in the process. If so, let's call those vital actions. Also consider whether any were examples of what we might call nonvital actions. These could be actions that you planned to do but ended up not doing in the service of avoiding difficult experiences. Or perhaps there were actions you did, but you did them in the service of avoiding difficult experiences; in the service of reasons; in the service of proving something to yourself or others; or even just in the service of not wanting to be unsuccessful in following through. It's okay if some of your actions felt nonvital. After all, you're still taking your first steps toward your valued life.

Now use this worksheet (also in appendix I) to jot down the actions you undertook. For each action, indicate whether you think it was vital or nonvital by writing an X in the appropriate column. Next, indicate whether you felt that each action created a sense of expansion in your life or a sense of contraction, again by writing an X in the appropriate column. You can use this worksheet to keep track of your actions throughout the week and identify whether they create a sense of vitality and expansion.

◆　◆　◆

BOLD MOVE

(Martin Wilks, 2013)

While most clients can name values such as acting and living with love, freedom, loyalty, and honor, some have difficulty defining what moving in the direction of these values would look like in their lives. One strategy for helping clients envision how these values and their related goals would look is to playfully generate a list of projects that would give full expression to a value. The projects can be anything at all, as long as they involve action and not just thought. Work together with clients to come up with a list of projects. Keep the process of generating these projects playful, but also encourage clients to discover doable bold moves and to use defusion and acceptance strategies to address barriers. Here's an example of projects a therapist might suggest to support a value of living life with a sense of freedom:

You could define freedom as creative freedom and set aside every Saturday morning to work on a creative project, with the commitment that in three months you'll deliver the result to someone, somewhere, without apology.

You could define freedom as time freedom and make a plan that will allow you to work just four days a week, or work one day from home.

You could define freedom as physical freedom and set yourself the challenge of climbing some of the highest peaks in your region next year.

You could define freedom as autonomy and come up with a project to earn money from something that excites you. This can start small—for example, selling cards online or to friends. But your plan could be scalable—for example, creating a website (very easy) or blog (really easy) to sell things from.

The client is likely to say that some of the projects are impossible. Take this as an opportunity to discuss how the mind tends to immediately give reasons why various goals aren't possible. Encourage the client to thank the mind—after all, it's just trying to keep him safe—and then carry on. Remind the client that although he can't control his thoughts, he can control his choices.

Committed Action Metaphors

While the nuts-and-bolts work of identifying values, goals, and actions is clear and seldom requires illustration, you can use metaphor to highlight the link between values and goals, the evolving nature of committed action, the sense of openness and acceptance that's required, and the vitality and growth that values-based living can create.

◆ ◆ ◆

THE TRAVELING PARTNERS

(Niloofar Afari, 2013)

Similar to the metaphors Passengers on the Bus and Joe the Bum (Hayes et al., 1999, pp. 157–158, and 239–240), the Traveling Partners metaphor can be used to explore willingness and choice and how they're related to committed action. This metaphor focuses on choice, forward movement, and making room for unwanted experiences.

Imagine that traveling has always been your dream and now you're going to live that dream. You've planned a trip around the world. For several years you've spent a lot of time reading about all of the countries you want to visit, the best attractions to see, where to stay, what to eat, and how to get from one place to another. You've spent a lot of money at a top-notch travel agency to book your tour.

Finally the big day arrives. You show up to the airport to get on your plane and begin your amazing adventure. As you walk down the jetway, you begin to notice that the other passengers are a motley group of people—some with dirty hair, some who smell, some who have missing teeth, some who smoke, and so on. These are going to be your traveling partners on your fabulous around-the-world tour. Now you have a choice to make: Are you going to turn around, go home, and miss out on an opportunity of a lifetime? Or are you going to get on the plane with these traveling partners and go see the world?

Let's say you choose to get on the plane, but you tell yourself that you're going to ignore your traveling partners and keep to yourself. That works somewhat when you're on the plane and can pretend to read or sleep so you don't have to interact with your traveling partners. But then you get to the first destination and the whole group goes to see a famous statue. You've been waiting your whole life to see this statue. As your traveling partners rush ahead to take a good look, you hang back so you don't have to interact with them. As a result, you only get a brief glance at part of the statue.

You have a choice to make here too: Are you going to keep hanging back and avoiding your traveling partners—and keep missing out on fully experiencing everything this trip has to offer? Or are you going to keep up with the group, say hello or in some way acknowledge your traveling partners, and get to see all the sites at their best? This is your choice for the entire trip.

♦ ♦ ♦

WAITING FOR THE WRONG TRAIN

(Aidan Hart, 2006)

The metaphor of Waiting for the Wrong Train is designed to work on the feeling of stuckness that can keep clients from moving in the direction of their values. For example, some clients can get stuck on the idea that they can't act on their values until things get better or until something undesired is no longer present.

Imagine you're going on a journey. The destination is somewhere really special, a place you really want to visit—somewhere you've wanted to go for as long as you can remember. When you get to the train station, you see two trains, both of them with signs for your chosen destination. One is a bit odd looking and strange. Some of the seats look hard and uncomfortable, and overall it looks kind of dirty. The train on the next platform is quite different. It looks familiar, safe, and reliable. The sign says it has air-conditioning, a cinema, and a fancy dining car with free, all-you-can-eat French cuisine. You think, Wow! I just have to take this train. I couldn't possibly make my journey on that other one—no way!

So you wait to board the wonderful train, and in the meanwhile the odd-looking train goes on its way. You keep waiting for the safe, comfortable train to board, and in the meanwhile, another odd train leaves the station, and then another, and another. All the while, you're waiting for a chance to board this great, reliable train so you can take your journey. But here's the thing: What if the safe train won't ever leave the station? What if you're waiting for the wrong train?

The main purpose of this metaphor is to draw attention to the process of moving forward even with difficulty versus being stuck even if stuck in relative comfort. You can ask the following questions to further explore the issues raised by the metaphor:

How does waiting for the good old predictable train work in terms of actually moving toward your values and goals?

If you can't ever have discomfort, where does that leave you?

You know where you want to go in life. What are you prepared to have or experience to get there?

◆ ◆ ◆

THE ROPE BRIDGE

(David Gillanders, 2013)

The metaphor of the Rope Bridge is useful when clients have a clear idea of their values and goals but are struggling with psychological barriers that prevent movement, such as anxiety and fear. The metaphor was developed for use in the context of partner relationships where fear of rejection may stand in the way of building greater intimacy.

> *So, here you are: You've been able to acknowledge that there's something you long for—greater connection and intimacy with your partner—and as you get in touch with that, a lot of fear comes up for you. There are a lot of thoughts about whether you should put yourself out there:* What if he rejects me? What if things get worse?
>
> *This would be a little like you standing up on a high cliff overlooking a narrow, deep canyon. You can see something you really want on the other side of the canyon. You can see a place where you could really live, where you would be connected with and loved by your partner. And you can see that there's a way to get to the other side of the canyon. It's an old rope bridge right in front of you. As you look at it, you aren't sure the bridge is totally safe. Maybe there are a few planks missing. Maybe it looks a bit worn. But you also aren't sure that it definitely isn't safe. And there on the other side is the place where you really want to be.*
>
> *If this really were the situation, what choices would you have?*

Take the time to process this metaphor, examining all of the different choices and possibilities. For example, the client could decide that the bridge isn't safe and therefore be unwilling to take the risk of stepping on it. In that case, it's clear that there isn't going to be any movement. She's staying put. Alternatively, the she could decide to just go for it and run across the bridge hoping that she'll get to the other side. That move might work, yet there's also the possibility that the bridge isn't safe and the client will fall. Another option is to move cautiously, for example, putting one foot on the bridge to test it while keeping the other foot on solid ground. A key to this discussion is to help the client recognize that it isn't possible to find out if the bridge is safe or not while standing still.

◆　　◆　　◆

WALKING THE PATH

(David Gillanders, 2013)

The metaphor of Walking the Path is useful for clients who are struggling to maintain new behaviors and are being pulled back into older, more avoidant and fused forms of relating.

> *The work that we're doing here is like walking across a wild hillside. This work is brand new, so there's no path to walk on. Every step may be effortful, and deliberate effort is needed to keep taking steps. Then you look over to your right and see a well-worn path. It looks like it would be so much easier to walk on that path than to keep persisting on this unmarked route across the tall, overgrown grass.*
>
> *The thing is, you know exactly where that well-worn path goes because you've walked it so many times before. Where does that path lead in your life?*

Give the client some time to reflect on this and get in touch with the unworkability of previous agendas. Help the client link this with creative hopelessness.

> *So, here we are.* (Consider physically moving to sit beside the client or using your hands to indicate a sense of being side by side.) *We're walking together across new territory, and sometimes it's not so easy. Then you see that old, familiar path… What have you learned from our work together that could be useful to you in those moments when you notice that you're being pulled onto that old familiar path? What will it take for this new path to eventually become well-worn and easier to walk on?*

Use defusion and acceptance interventions to help the client identify ways to remain on the new path, then return the focus to the values-based element of the work.

> *Let's spend a moment noticing and contacting the direction this new path is traveling. Where does this new path lead? What are some of the things we could see along this new path?*

♦ ♦ ♦

THE BICYCLE FACTORY

(David Gillanders, 2013)

The metaphor of the Bicycle Factory was developed to help clients maintain behavior change after the termination of therapy. Therefore, it's useful toward the end of therapy. It's especially applicable to situations where ongoing management of a condition is required, such as chronic illness, but it can also be used in other situations to emphasize the importance of continued commitment to skills practice.

Imagine a small factory that makes hand-built bicycles. There are various work stations on the production line. Some people are welding frames together, others are painting them, others are assembling wheels and components, others are putting the pieces together, and there's even a person who comes around with a snack tray at break times.

There's also a manager in this factory. What kinds of jobs would the manager do?

Give the client some time to list potential management tasks. If need be, offer suggestions such as generating sales, ordering parts, making sure people get paid, making sure things run smoothly, and so on.

Now, importantly, the manager doesn't actually make the bikes, but she does have an overview of the whole place. In fact, the manager's office sits above the factory floor so that she can monitor everything by looking out over the whole production line. (Use additional language and hand gestures to emphasize the hierarchical relationship between the manager and the production line.) *The manager has this overview so she can see trouble brewing and intervene. She works persistently at ongoing management of the whole process, and her continuous attention keeps things running well.*

Now imagine that in this factory everything is going extremely well. Orders are up, bikes are being made and shipped, quality is good, everyone is getting paid, and the workers are contented. There's even a great choice of snacks on the snack tray. And imagine if the manager were to look at all of this and say, "Things are going so well. I'm going to take six months off and go to the Bahamas." What do you think things will look like by the time she comes back?

165

Give the client time to list a variety of problems that may have arisen. If need be, offer suggestions such as parts not being ordered, workers not being paid, bad morale due to ongoing arguments, a downturn in sales, running out of snacks, and so on.

So, this treatment we've been doing isn't like some other treatments you may have had. For example, if you have an infection, you might go to the doctor and get a prescription for an antibiotic. You're expected to take the medication, but once the infection is gone, you don't need to keep doing anything. This treatment isn't like that. In here, you've been learning how to live life with your difficulties, and the continuous, flexible attention you've been devoting to that is like the manager's careful attention to the factory.

Now, when the manager has her factory functioning nicely, she can perhaps afford to work only part-time, just keeping an eye on things for a while each day and spending the rest of her time relaxing. But she still needs to give the factory some attention regularly and not let things slide. How does this strike you?

Spend some time discussing what's meaningful to clients in maintaining the gains made in therapy and continuing to build larger patterns of committed action. The Bicycle Factory metaphor can also help clients anticipate the relapses and setbacks that are likely to occur.

Summary

Committed action refers to purposeful behavior change in the service of chosen values, with a willingness to experience the thoughts, feelings, and reactions that show up in the process of moving forward. The work in committed action centers on identifying and undertaking goals and action plans that link with clients' values while staying alert to experiential and environmental barriers that may lead clients away from values-based action. In this chapter, we reviewed the core concept of committed action and discussed many of the issues that can arise as clients commit to pursuing valued goals.

We also provided metaphors and exercises that draw out the link between values and goals and the evolving nature of committed action—metaphors and exercises that highlight the sense of openness and acceptance that's necessary for committed action and the vitality and growth that can follow from values-based living. We also included a few interventions that address the pull to fall back into old, avoidant patterns of behavior. The key question when examining behavior change is whether clients are moving toward values or away from unwanted experiences. Work with clients to help them apply this question to any behavior change that arises during the course of therapy. With time and practice, clients will be able to address this question on their own with greater skill.

◆ ◆ ◆

Metaphors and Exercises Targeting Committed Action

Metaphors and Exercises in This Chapter

- Zorg the Alien
- The Bubble
- Bold Move
- The Traveling Partners
- Waiting for the Wrong Train
- The Rope Bridge
- Walking the Path
- The Bicycle Factory

In addition, the following exercises and metaphors, available in the sources cited, also target committed action.

Other Exercises

- Eye Contact (Hayes et al., 1999, pp. 244–245)
- Right-Wrong Game (Walser & Westrup, 2007, pp. 176–178)
- Stand and Commit (Walser & Westrup, 2007, pp. 190–191)
- Trying vs. Doing (Zettle, 2007, p. 129)

- We Are All in This Together (Walser & Westrup, 2007, pp. 162–164)

Other Metaphors

- Basketball Game (Luoma et al., 2007, pp. 166–167)

- Bubble in the Road (Hayes et al., 1999, pp. 229–230)

- Expanding Circle (Luoma et al., 2007, pp. 167–168)

- Skidding (Luoma et al., 2007, p. 170)

CHAPTER 9

BRINGING IT ALL TOGETHER

Metaphor is an essential feature of human communication. All cultures and religions use stories, anecdotes, and parables to convey specific messages, improve understanding, and suggest action. Metaphors also have a long history of use in building rapport, decreasing resistance, increasing motivation, reframing problems and solutions, and bringing about psychotherapeutic change (Gordon, 1978; Rosen, 1982; Barker, 1985). Likewise, various forms of psychotherapy have used experiential techniques that focus on present-moment awareness to explore clients' relationships with self and others (Perls, Hefferline, & Goodman, 1951; Polster & Polster, 1973; Kabat-Zinn, 1991).

The Role of Metaphors and Exercises in ACT

While the use of metaphors and exercises in psychotherapy isn't unique to ACT, there are several characteristics of ACT that make its use of metaphors and exercises novel. First, ACT conceptualizes psychological inflexibility as a product of language. If language is part of the problem, then how does therapy, which relies heavily on verbal communication, bypass the ill effects of language? ACT's use of metaphors and experiential techniques is specifically intended to bring clients into direct contact with experience as well as to undermine the adverse effects of language in general and verbal instructions in therapy in particular. Second, ACT's grounding in behavior analysis and RFT makes it possible to examine the basic science underlying the benefits of metaphor use. While a scientific review of the processes by which metaphor and experiential techniques can lead to behavior change is outside the scope of this book, chapter 2 provided a concise summary of the RFT account of metaphor as an experiential tool. Third, and lastly, as the structure of this book suggests, ACT's use of metaphors and experiential exercises is situated in the context of each of ACT's six core therapeutic processes; that is, the ACT model uses metaphors and exercises in a particular context to serve a particular purpose based on a functional analytic conceptualization of what the individual client is struggling with.

In this final chapter, we tie up loose ends by providing some general guidelines on how to best use metaphors and exercises in the context of ACT, regardless of the core therapeutic process being targeted. Additionally, we orient you toward additional resources here and in the appendices that could be used together with this book to enhance your practice of ACT.

General Guidelines for Use of Metaphors and Exercises in ACT

In chapters 3 through 8, we provided descriptions and scripts for metaphors and exercises that target each of the ACT therapeutic processes. The introduction to each exercise or metaphor addresses the related therapeutic processes, creating context to help you choose what to use when. However, the ACT model isn't about choosing the "perfect" metaphor or exercise or about using a large number of metaphors and exercises strung together to communicate with the client. Rather, metaphors and exercises are merely tools, and they work best if used flexibly to fit the needs, struggles, and history of individual clients.

Since ACT is more than a compilation of metaphors and exercises, it's essential for therapists to build competency with ACT through experiential workshops and studying the literature. We've found the book *Learning ACT* (Luoma et al., 2007) to be an excellent guide to learning the principles of ACT, building therapeutic skills, and recognizing how and when metaphors and exercises fit into ACT clinical practice. It also provides excellent advice on avoiding common pitfalls.

We heartily recommend that you turn to other resources for a thorough grounding in ACT, so here we'll provide just a few general guidelines for situating metaphors and exercises in the course of therapy. We'll also offer some recommendations on how to best use these ACT approaches.

Situating Metaphors and Exercises

Our first set of guidelines focuses on your stance as a therapist. What you do to establish a therapeutic relationship, the agenda you bring into the session, and your willingness to go outside of your comfort zone in conducting therapy can make a big difference in client responses to metaphors and exercises.

Build a therapeutic alliance and conduct a functional analysis. As with any other form of therapy, the building blocks of successful engagement are establishing rapport, building a therapeutic relationship, and developing a deep understanding of what the client is struggling with by means of functional analysis. Within the ACT model, these building blocks are essential for accurately targeting the relevant ACT processes, and for the therapist to actively engage clients in goals and tasks that differ from what they may have expected. A genuine and understanding relationship also can facilitate the use of playful and irreverent metaphors and exercises, as well as interventions that elicit difficult thoughts, emotions, and other private events.

Hold your agenda lightly. Allow the context of the session and the client's behavior to influence your responses. In other words, attend to the function of the client's behavior in session and respond accordingly by choosing appropriate metaphors and exercises and tailoring them to specific clients and their struggles. There are many standard metaphors and exercises in the various ACT protocols, and this book has added to the collection. It can be tempting, especially for beginning ACT therapists, to rely heavily on these techniques and pack several into a session based on a protocol or agenda. However, overreliance on metaphors and exercises in the absence of an ACT-consistent context or without connection to the client's experience can lead to confusion at best, and client disengagement and premature termination at worst. It's important for the therapist to stay in the present moment in session to better attend to clients' behavior and verbal and nonverbal responses and make room for the processing of experiences and emotions. Let clients' comments and responses evoke particular metaphors and exercises.

Be open to taking risks. While therapists who learn about ACT generally connect well with the model, many find it anxiety provoking to use the tools and techniques that are new to them. Particularly for beginning therapists, it isn't uncommon to avoid defusion or self-as-context techniques, for example, because they fall outside the norm of general communication and are perceived as difficult to understand. Others find it difficult to lead eyes-closed exercises and may avoid their own feelings of anxiety or thoughts (e.g., *This is stupid, and I don't know what I'm doing*) by merely explaining the concepts underlying the exercises rather than conducting them experientially. The challenge for ACT therapists is to examine their own patterns of behavioral and psychological avoidance, clarify what they value in their roles as therapists, and willingly make some bold moves in using metaphors and exercises that they aren't accustomed to. After all, taking gradually larger risks is what we are often asking clients to do.

How to Best Use Metaphors and Exercises

Now we'll provide a few guidelines on the nuts and bolts of using metaphors and exercises in the most effective manner.

Be prepared. Take time to prepare, reading and becoming familiar with the metaphors and exercises that you plan to use in session and their intended purpose. It's helpful to practice by reading aloud so you can become comfortable with both the content and the tone and pace of your voice when you present a metaphor or exercise in session. It can also be useful to practice an exercise with yourself or others (e.g., friends, relatives, or colleagues) to get an experiential understanding of what clients may experience or report in response to the exercise. Although it's tempting to take scripts into sessions and read from them, doing so is distracting and can also covertly feed both your own rule-following agenda and the client's. Becoming familiar enough with the content and intent of each metaphor and exercise to offer it from memory allows for a more flexible and experiential therapeutic context—one in which you can be attentive to the needs of the client and the therapeutic interaction in the moment.

Personalize your approach. To the extent possible, use the client's own language, history, preferences, and personal struggles to customize metaphors and exercises. For example, you can incorporate what you know of the client's thoughts and feelings into an exercise or tweak a client's story about an activity or event within a metaphor. Using clients' cultural background or personal experience can also help them better see the link between the metaphor and their own situation. In addition, it can facilitate experiential contact with consequences observed in the metaphor that are relevant to the individual's situation.

Resist the pull of explanations. Beware of the potential pitfall of trying to explain the meaning of metaphors and exercises. Clients often seek a logical understanding of an experience. In response, therapists can fall into the trap of wanting to help clients "get it." This trap can be especially prominent when working with defusion and self-as-context, with which the desire for literal understanding can be strong. It's important to recognize that information gathering and making literal sense of an experience often function as yet more experiential avoidance for both clients and therapists. Keep in mind that metaphors and exercises are used to bring clients into closer contact with experiential knowing versus verbal or logical knowing. Therefore, getting it will probably look different than being able to verbally state a summary of what the experience was about. It may involve silence, tears, or other displays of emotion.

Seek client permission. Give clients an opportunity to practice choice and willingness by asking permission before launching into a metaphor or exercise, especially one that may evoke strong or unpleasant thoughts, feelings, or bodily sensations. This could be something as simple as "What we're talking about right now reminds me of X (e.g., a chessboard, driving a bus, steering a sailboat). Would it be okay if we took a few minutes to unpack that?" Or you might simply say, "Would you be willing to do an exercise with me that might be helpful?"

Addressing Multiple ACT Processes

In organizing this book, we chose to categorize the metaphors and exercises according to the six core therapeutic processes. However, many of the metaphors and exercises contain elements that are relevant to multiple ACT processes. Our approach was to highlight the primary function of each metaphor or exercise but also identify those that address multiple processes. We sometimes included supplemental text that can be used to demonstrate additional processes. We also provided several scripts for metaphors that bring most or all of the processes together. These are often used in the latter part of therapy when clients are working on building larger patterns of effective action.

Alternatively, some metaphors that have elements of nearly all of the core processes are best used toward the beginning of therapy in order to set the context or direction of the therapeutic work. A great example of this is the metaphor the Sailing Boat, created by David Gillanders.

◆　◆　◆

THE SAILING BOAT
(David Gillanders, 2013)

The metaphor of the Sailing Boat addresses workability and creative hopelessness, values, acceptance, and committed action. It can be used early in treatment to highlight the unworkability of efforts to change thoughts, feelings, and other private events and reveal the dominance of the problem-solving mind. Additionally, it hints at acceptance and values-based action as the course the treatment will take.

Imagine that life is like sailing a small sailing boat. During your life, you've picked up the skills necessary to sail your boat and you have a sense of where you're taking it. At some point in learning how to sail, you discovered that, from time to time, waves may wash over the bow, getting your feet wet. The usual response is to use a bailer to bail out the water, and like most people, you've learned about the bailer.

Now, most of the time the bailer is stored in a locker, ready to be used if needed. And at some point along your journey, waves come over your boat. Now there's water in the bottom of your boat. So you've started to do the thing that's sensible and logical to do: get rid of the water. You've been using that bailer a lot, sometimes bailing quickly, sometimes bailing carefully, sometimes bailing wildly, sometimes bailing desperately. In your experience, have you managed to get rid of the water yet? (You can elaborate here; for example, there may be passengers or crew on the boat who are also shouting directions and giving their two cents on how the client should get rid of the water.)

And all of this time, as you've been bailing, what has been happening to the direction and progress your boat has been making? Is it fair to say that you've been bailing more than you've been sailing the boat?

Now what if one day you really look at the bailer and see that it's full of holes? What if it's actually a sieve? What would you have to do? (Most clients recognize that a sieve isn't a good bailer and suggest using a different tool, like a bucket or their hands.)

Well, it may be that part of the work we do together is about investigating which tools are really useful to you. Some of them may be more effective for bailing.

Even more than that, the implicit promise of bailing is this: once you get rid of the water, then you'll get your boat back on track and start sailing it where you want to go. What if our work could really be about that—about working together to let go of needing to get rid of the water, to begin looking up from the bailing and actually choosing a direction in which you want to travel? What if our work could be about helping you put a hand on the tiller and choosing to pull in the sails—about getting the boat moving in whatever direction you choose? This could occur slowly at first; there's no speedometer in this work. Once we get the boat moving, then we might be able to investigate some other ways of bailing—if they prove to be useful strategies in helping you to take the boat where you want it to go.

The question to ask yourself might be something like this: if you could have only a little water in the bottom of the boat but you'd be adrift without a direction, or if the boat had water in the bottom, maybe sometimes so much water that you'd wonder how it was still afloat, but you were still taking this boat, however slowly, in the direction you most want to take it, which would you choose?

To highlight the behavioral nature of the treatment and the goal of committed action, you can use the following addition, which focuses on how a small course adjustment can develop into big changes over time.

Imagine that you were able to make a small course change, turning just five degrees closer to the direction in life that you'd most like to travel. Now, such a course adjustment may be unnoticeable at first, but if you were able to stick to that small course change, over the course of thousands of miles your boat would be very far from where it would have been otherwise.

You can draw a diagram like this to support the idea.

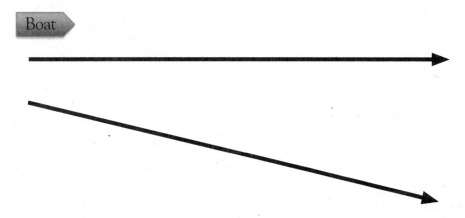

Throughout the presentation of this metaphor, take the time to explore the client's reactions and ask questions about what thoughts and emotions are showing up in relation to this scenario. Also incorporate the client's perspective into the scenario. For example, some clients may suggest that their problem isn't that there's water in the boat, but that the boat is being dragged or slowed down by an anchor, which is essentially a description of their problem. Because the anchor and the water in the boat are functionally equivalent in terms of hampering travel in a chosen direction, you can just incorporate the anchor into the metaphor by saying something like "So what you've been trying to get rid of is the anchor."

Another consideration is that clients sometimes generate strategies that they may evaluate as more effective ways of bailing. For example, clients who experience physical pain may find certain pain-control strategies that are sometimes effective and can be helpful. In these instances, it's important to focus the metaphor and the ACT work more generally, on workability, flexibility, and behavior in the service of growing a life, rather than on eliminating or controlling experiences. In the case of chronic pain, taking medication may function to eliminate pain temporarily, or it may help the client be able to attend her son's baseball game.

As with all of the exercises and metaphors in this book, we encourage you to use the Sailing Boat metaphor flexibly, adapting or adding to it in ways that will work best for specific clients.

Other Resources

Our focus in this book was novel metaphors and experiential exercises that have been developed or adapted specifically for use within the ACT model. The book is by no means exhaustive. A simple search on Google or Amazon can generate a lengthy list of books and materials from various traditions, some of which we have referenced in this book. Many of these previously published materials are consistent with the ACT model or can easily be adapted to fit one or more of the ACT core principles.

Of course, the growing list of ACT-specific books begins with *Acceptance and Commitment Therapy: An Experiential Approach to Behavior Change*, the seminal book by Steven Hayes and colleagues (1999) that describes a number of foundational metaphors and exercises and provides scripts for many of them. For a listing of these and other classic ACT interventions, see appendix J. Although the list in appendix J isn't comprehensive, it does include many of the essential ACT metaphors and exercises that have been previously published. Our hope is that this list will make it easier for you to find the classic ACT metaphors and exercises not included here.

Most prominent among recommended resources from outside the ACT community are books by Tara Brach (e.g., *Radical Acceptance*, 2003, and *True Refuge*, 2013) and Jon Kabat-Zinn (e.g., *Full Catastrophe Living*, 1991, and *Mindfulness for Beginners*, 2011). Because ACT and dialectical behavior therapy share many common features, materials designed for dialectical behavior therapy also can be easily adapted for use within ACT. Frequently cited examples include *Skills Training Manual for Treating Borderline Personality Disorder* (Linehan, 1993b) and *The Dialectical Behavior Therapy Skills Workbook* (McKay, Wood, & Brantley, 2007).

We recommend that you use this book as an adjunct to other, more comprehensive books and protocols. Our goal in writing this book was to expand the array of metaphors and exercises available for use within the ACT framework. Although we've provided background information on each of the six core therapeutic processes, our focus was on building a resource for handy reference, rather than introducing and teaching ACT. The Resources section provides a selected list of publications that comprehensively address ACT's conceptualization of psychological inflexibility and experiential avoidance and its larger framework as an experiential approach to behavior change.

Conclusion

ACT is an approach to psychological intervention that's based on basic behavioral principles and a behavioral theory of language: RFT. The ACT model postulates that language processes are at the core of psychological and behavioral inflexibility, and therefore at the root of human suffering. The overarching goal of ACT is to undermine language processes in ways that improve people's ability to contact the present moment more fully and with awareness, and that allow them to undertake or persist in behavior that moves them in valued directions. Six core therapeutic processes—acceptance, defusion, present-moment awareness, self-as-context, values, and committed action—are used to engender psychological and behavioral flexibility. Metaphors and experiential exercises play a central role in ACT, helping undermine the adverse effects of language by creating contexts in which clients can have more direct and experiential contact with the consequences of valued-driven action.

With a grounding in RFT and an understanding of each of the six core therapeutic processes, anyone can create ACT-consistent metaphors and exercises. The novel and powerful metaphors and exercises developed by members of the ACT community that are included in this book are a testament to that. This book offers a collection of tools and techniques that can enhance your application of ACT and embolden your clients to live a valued life. We hope that it also empowers you to develop and share your own unique and personal metaphors and exercises.

Appendix A

Mindfulness Diary

Jessica Gundy Cuneo

Over the next week, choose three to five different time periods to complete this form. Be sure to fill in all of the information each time. Here are the steps for using the form:

1. Choose a mindfulness activity to engage in.

2. Prior to beginning the exercise, decide on a specific time and place where you will do this mindfulness practice. This may be a quiet place with no distractions or, conversely, a place where distractions are likely to occur.

3. Just before beginning the activity, note any inner experiences you may be having: thoughts, feelings, physical sensations, or memories.

4. Note how long you practiced.

5. Did anything help, hinder, or interfere with doing the practice?

A downloadable copy of this form can be found at http://www.newharbinger.com/25295.

What mindfulness activity will you do?	When and where will you do it?	What inner experiences are you having before beginning?	What was the duration of the activity?	Did anything help or hinder your mindfulness practice?

APPENDIX B

ACT THOUGHT RECORD

Elizabeth Maher

The purpose of this diary form is to help you become increasingly aware of the feelings and thoughts that show up in a variety of situations you experience throughout the week, and to give you the opportunity to practice acceptance and present-moment awareness strategies and choose actions that are in line with your values. Over the next week, choose three to five different situations to examine with this form. Be sure to fill in all of the information each time.

1. Briefly describe the situation.

2. Record the feelings you notice, including emotions and physical sensations.

3. Record the thoughts going through your mind as you are in the situation.

4. Practice one of the present-moment awareness exercises that help with observing inner experience, recognizing thoughts as thoughts and feeling as feelings. Note any responses you have to allowing thoughts and feelings to come and go.

5. Take a few moments to identify your values that are salient in this situation.

6. Choose an action or response that's in line with your values.

A downloadable copy of the diary form can be found at http://www.newharbinger .com/25295.

Situation	Feelings	Thoughts	Present-moment awareness	Values	Action

APPENDIX C

MUSIC MINDFULNESS AND DEFUSION HANDOUT

Levin Schwartz

A copy of this resource is available for download at http://www.newharbinger.com/25295.

MUSIC, MINDFULNESS & DEFUSION

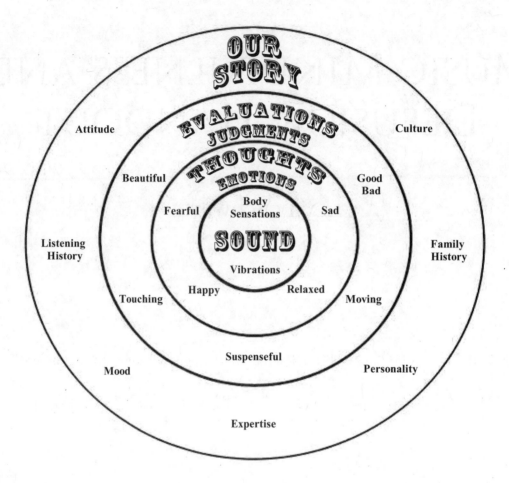

This diagram represents an example of how we can become fused with our thoughts. The experience of listening to music can provoke many powerful sensations, thoughts, experiences, evaluations, and judgments. Consider that this is exactly what our minds do—this is programming and it is happening all the time.

At the center of the circle is the musical event that represents "just the facts" of "what actually happened." The further away the circles are from the musical event, the more variable and subjective the emotions become. This process accounts for the individual variables and factors influencing our experience, which make up "our story."

Appendix D

Values Words

Nicole Rensenbrink

Below is a list of words that may help you generate ideas about your values. Note that some of these words, like Calm, Patience, and Courage, may refer to internal experiences. In these cases, the value may be to *act* calmly or with patience or courage, even if you don't feel this way. The value should *not* be to achieve an internal feeling state. A copy of this resource is available for download at http://www.newharbinger.com/25295.

Adventure	Expansiveness	Love	Self-sufficiency
Attentiveness	Experience	Loyalty	Sensuality
Balance	Faith	Magic	Serenity
Beauty	Fitness	Meaning	Simplicity
Belonging	Flow	Nesting	Spirituality
Calm	Forgiveness	Nurturance	Spontaneity
Caring	Freedom	Openness	Stability
Citizenship	Fun	Order	Stewardship
Comfort	Health	Organization	Strength
Communication	Honor	Patience	Structure
Compassion	Humor	Peace	Sustainability
Connectedness	Imagination	Perseverance	Thoughtfulness
Conservation	Independence	Play	Tolerance
Courage	Integrity	Power	Transcendence
Creativity	Intelligence	Productivity	Understanding
Curiosity	Interdependence	Reliability	Warmth
Detachment	Intimacy	Respect	Wisdom
Discipline	Intuition	Reverence	Wit
Diversity	Justice	Rhythm	Wonder
Effort	Kindness	Risk	
Equality	Leadership	Security	
Excitement	Learning	Self-expression	

APPENDIX E

THE HEROES EXERCISE WORKSHEET

Rob Archer

Think about who your heroes are and choose a few people you admire. These may be people you know, celebrities, or even fictional characters. On the following sheet, write in the columns provided:

1. The name of your hero

2. The values this person embodies that you admire

3. Actions you can take to start moving in the direction of being more like this person

4. Obstacles you anticipate (e.g., thoughts, feelings, urges, memories) that might get in the way of your committed actions

5. Skills and/or exercises you might use to handle obstacles so that you can keep your feet moving toward being more like your hero

A downloadable copy of this form can be found at http://www.newharbinger.com /25295.

My heroes	What I admire (values)	How I can move toward being more like my hero (committed action)	Obstacles I anticipate (thoughts, feelings, memories, urges, etc.)	What I can do to move forward anyway (like my hero would!)
Example: Oprah Winfrey	Perseverance, assertiveness, being genuine	Go after the new job. Tell my partner how I feel.	Fear that I'm not good enough to land the job. Fear that my partner will get mad or leave me.	Mindfulness and defusion. The Bold Move

WRITING YOUR AUTOBIOGRAPHY WORKSHEET

Mark Stern

A downloadable copy of this resource can be found at http://www.newharbinger.com /25295.

After taking ample time to think about your autobiography as it would appear after you've lived a truly meaningful, fulfilling life that was full of vitality, write down the values that were expressed through your personal story.

_____

_____

_____

_____

_____

_____

After taking time to think about your autobiography as it would appear if it were written about you today, write down what showed up.

_____

_____

_____

_____

_____

_____

_____

Now write a few thoughts about any discrepancies that arose when comparing your ideal autobiography to your present-day story.

_____

_____

_____

_____

_____

_____

_____

APPENDIX G

VALUES AND COMMITTED ACTION WORKSHEET

Jill Stoddard

Find a downloadable copy of this worksheet at http://www.newharbinger.com/25295.

Area of importance	How I want to be	Things I can do	What might get in my way	How I can move forward	Exercises
Physical health	*Treat my body with love and respect*	*Commit to yoga twice a week; walk my dog daily; eat fruits and vegetables with every meal*	*Feeling lazy, unmotivated; thinking "What's the point, I always fail"*	*Acceptance, defusion, staying connected to bigger values*	*Crying Baby on a Plane; Watching the Mind Train; The Heroes*

Appendix H

The Classroom Professor Graphics and Worksheet

Jill Stoddard

Downloadable copies of these materials are available at http://www.newharbinger.com /25295.

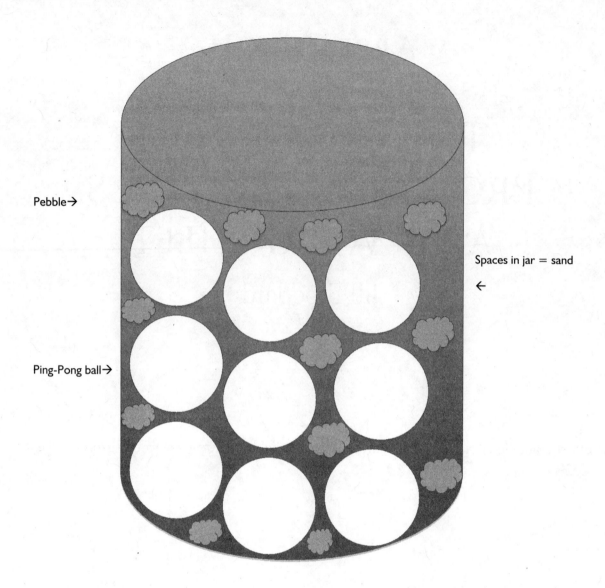

Pebble→

Spaces in jar = sand
←

Ping-Pong ball→

Ping-Pong Balls

1. _____

2. _____

3. _____

4. _____

5. _____

6. _____

7. _____

8. _____

Small Rocks

1. _____

2. _____

3. _____

4. _____

5. _____

6. _____

7. _____

8. _____

Sand

1. _____

2. _____

3. _____

4. _____

5. _____

6. _____

7. _____

8. _____

APPENDIX I

THE BUBBLE EXERCISE GRAPHICS AND WORKSHEET

Nuno Ferreira

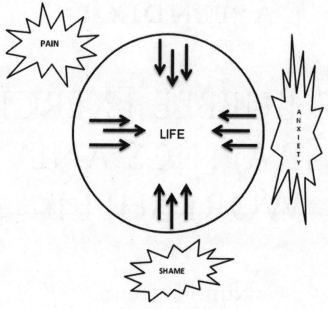

Figure 1. Life Contraction

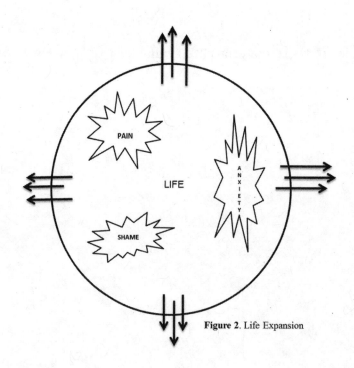

Figure 2. Life Expansion

The Bubble Exercise Worksheet

In the columns below, list committed actions you took over the past week in the "Action" column. Place an X in the "Vital" column for actions completed in the service of values, and place an X in the "Nonvital" column to those completed (or not completed) in the service of avoidance. Next, place an X in the "Expansion" or "Contraction" columns to indicate whether the action created a sense of expansion and vitality in your life, or one of contraction or limitation.

Action	Vital	Nonvital	Expansion	Contraction

APPENDIX J

SELECTED LIST OF ADDITIONAL EXERCISES AND METAPHORS PUBLISHED ELSEWHERE

The ACT literature is replete with exercises and metaphors. Here, we've compiled a list of some of those that are most often used or cited. We've tried to cite the earliest published ACT version in most cases. This list also includes the handful of the exercises and metaphors in this book that have previously been published and appear here in adapted form with permission of the publisher.

Exercises and metaphors	Primary topic	Source
Exercises		
Accepting Yourself on Faith	Acceptance	Hayes et al., 1999, pp. 263–264
And/Be Out Convention	Defusion	Hayes et al., 1999, p. 167
Argyle Socks	Values	Hayes et al., 1999, pp. 211–212
Assessment of Values, Goals, Actions, and Barriers	Values	Hayes et al., 1999, pp. 222–223
Attending to Breathing	Present-moment awareness	Walser & Westrup, 2007, pp. 43–44
Attending Your Own Funeral	Values	Hayes, 2005, pp. 166–170

Be Mindful of Your Feet While You Read This	Present-moment awareness	Hayes, 2005, pp. 114–115
Be-Still Mindfulness	Present-moment awareness	Walser & Westrup, 2007, pp. 86–87
Be Where You Are	Present-moment awareness	Hayes, 2005, pp. 107–108
Being Willingly Out of Breath	Willingness	Hayes, 2005, pp. 49–51
Body Scan (with an ACT orientation)	Present-moment awareness	Walser & Westrup, 2007
Breathing Mindfully	Present-moment awareness	Zettle, 2007, pp. 143–144
Carrying Your Depression	Control as the problem	Zettle, 2007, pp. 110–111
Child	Acceptance	Walser & Westrup, 2007, pp. 186–188
Chinese Finger Cuffs	Control as the problem	Eifert & Forsyth, 2005, pp. 146–149
Chocolate Cake	Control as the problem	Hayes et al., 1999, pp. 124–125
Compassion Mindfulness	Acceptance	Walser & Westrup, 2007, pp. 141
Contents on Cards	Defusion	Hayes et al., 1999, p. 162
Cubbyholing	Present-moment awareness	Hayes, 2005, pp. 109–110
Describing Thoughts and Feelings	Defusion	Hayes, 2005, pp. 78–79
Don't Think About Your Thoughts	Control as the problem	Hayes, 2005, pp. 25–26
Drinking Tea	Present-moment awareness	Hayes, 2005, pp. 111–112
Eating Mindfully	Present-moment awareness	Hayes, 2005, pp. 112–113
Mindfully Eating Raisins	Present-moment awareness	Kabat-Zinn, 1991, pp. 27–29
Empty Chair	Acceptance	Hayes et al., 1999, pp. 257–258
Experientially, I'm Not That	Self-as-context	Hayes, 2005, pp. 97–98
Eye Contact	Committed action	Hayes et al., 1999, pp. 244–245
Feeling Good	Control as the problem	Hayes et al., 1999, p. 145
Finding-the-Center Mindfulness	Present-moment awareness	Walser & Westrup, 2007, pp. 113–114
Floating Leaves on a Moving Stream	Defusion	Hayes, 2005, pp. 76–77

Fusion with Self-Evaluations	Self-as-context	Luoma et al., 2007, p. 118
Gazing at the Clouds (with an ACT orientation)	Present-moment awareness	Zettle, 2007, pp. 145–146
Giving Your Target a Form	Acceptance	Hayes, 2005, pp. 138–140
Hands-On	Willingness	Walser & Westrup, 2007, pp. 89–90
Identifying Programming	Defusion	Hayes et al., 1999, pp. 143–144
Jump	Willingness	Hayes et al., 1999, pp. 240–241
Just Listening	Present-moment awareness	Walser & Westrup, 2007, p. 68
Just Sitting	Present-moment awareness	Hayes, 2005, pp. 116–118
Kiss the Earth with Your Feet	Present-moment awareness	Walser & Westrup, 2007, pp. 164–165
Label Parade	Self-as-context	Walser & Westrup, 2007, pp. 126–131
Labeling Your Thoughts	Defusion	Hayes, 2005, pp. 75–76
Letting Go of Identity	Self-as-context	Walser & Westrup, 2007, pp. 136–137
Listening to Classical Music	Present-moment awareness	Hayes, 2005, pp. 113–114
Looking for Mr. Discomfort	Willingness	Hayes et al., 1999, pp. 246–247
Mental Polarity	Self-as-context	Hayes et al., 1999, p. 190
Milk, Milk, Milk (with an ACT orientation)	Defusion	Hayes et al., 1999, pp. 154–156
Mind-Reading Machine	Values	Harris, 2009, p. 201
Observer	Self-as-context	Hayes et al., 1999, pp. 192–196
The Pain Is Gone, Now What?	Control as the problem	Hayes, 2005, pp. 14–15
Physicalizing	Defusion	Hayes et al., 1999, pp. 170–171
Pick an Identity…Any Identity	Self-as-context	Hayes et al., 1999, pp. 196–197
Place of Peace	Present-moment awareness	Walser & Westrup, 2007, pp. 142
Practicing Awareness of Your Experience	Present-moment awareness	Hayes et al., 1999, p. 179
Reasons for Depression	Defusion	Zettle, 2007, pp. 102, 176, 245–246

Recognizing Mind-Quality Mindfulness	Control as the problem	Walser & Westrup, 2007, pp. 112–113
Retelling Your Own Story	Self-as-context	Hayes, 2005, pp. 91–92
Revisiting Childhood Wishes	Values	Zettle, 2007, pp. 120–121
Revocalization	Defusion	Zettle, 2007, pp. 98–99
Right-Wrong Game	Committed action	Walser & Westrup, 2007, pp. 176–178
Rules of the Game	Control as the problem	Hayes et al., 1999, pp. 145–146
A Screw, a Toothbrush, and a Lighter	Control as the problem	Hayes, 2005, pp. 21–22
Silent Walking	Present-moment awareness	Hayes, 2005, p. 109
Sitting with Feelings	Willingness	Zettle, 2007, pp. 112–113
Soldiers in the Parade	Defusion	Hayes et al., 1999, pp. 158–162
Stand and Commit	Committed action	Walser & Westrup, 2007, pp. 190–191
Sweet Spot	Values	Wilson & DuFrene, 2008, p. 203–209
Taking Inventory	Defusion	Zettle, 2007, p. 99
Taking Your Mind for a Walk	Defusion	Hayes et al., 1999, pp. 162–163
Talking and Listening	Self-as-context	Harris, 2009, p. 177
Ten Steps to Trying on a Value	Values	Dahl, Plumb, Stewart, & Lundgren, 2009, pp. 164–165
Tin Can Monster	Willingness	Hayes et al., 1999, pp. 171–174
Tracking Your Thoughts in Time	Present-moment awareness	Hayes, 2005, pp. 100–101
Trying vs. Doing	Committed action	Zettle, 2007, p. 129
Watching the Mind-Train	Defusion	Hayes, 2005, pp. 66–68
We Are All in This Together	Committed action	Walser & Westrup, 2007, pp. 162–164
Welcome Anxiety	Willingness	Walser & Westrup, 2007, pp. 87–88
What Are the Numbers?	Control as the problem	Hayes et al., 1999, pp. 126–128

What Do You Want Your Life to Stand For? (aka Eulogy or Tombstone)	Values	Hayes et al., 1999, pp. 215–218
Yellow Jeep	Control as the problem	Hayes, 2005, pp. 24–25
Your Mind Is Not Your Friend	Defusion	Hayes et al., 1999, pp. 151–152
Your Suffering Inventory	Control as the problem	Hayes, 2005, pp. 12–13
Metaphors		
Bad Cup	Defusion	Hayes et al., 1999, pp. 168–169
Basketball Game	Committed action	Luoma et al., 2007, pp. 166–167
Box Full of Stuff	Control as the problem	Hayes et al., 1999, pp. 136–138
Bubble in the Road	Committed action	Hayes et al., 1999, pp. 229–230
Chessboard	Self-as-context	Hayes et al., 1999, pp. 190–192, 219, 268
Chinese Handcuffs	Control as the problem	Hayes et al., 1999, pp. 104–105
Compass	Values	Zettle, 2007, pp. 124–125
Expanding Balloon	Willingness	Hayes et al., 1999, p. 248
Expanding Circle	Committed action	Luoma et al., 2007, pp. 167–168
Falling in Love	Control as the problem	Zettle, 2007, pp. 170–171
Feedback Screech	Control as the problem	Hayes et al., 1999, p. 108
Fighting the Wave	Control as the problem	Walser & Westrup, 2007, pp. 75–76
Finding a Place to Sit	Defusion	Hayes et al., 1999, pp. 152–153
Flat Tire	Defusion	Zettle, 2007, p. 103
Gardening	Values	Hayes et al., 1999, pp. 219–220, 228
Hands as Thoughts	Defusion	Harris, 2009, p. 20
High School Sweetheart	Willingness	Hayes et al., 1999, p. 252
Hungry Tiger	Control as the problem	Hayes, 2005, pp. 36–37
Joe the Bum	Willingness	Hayes et al., 1999, pp. 239–240
Magic Pill	Values	Zettle, 2007, pp. 197–198
Man in the Hole	Control as the problem	Hayes et al., 1999, pp. 101–104
Master Storyteller	Defusion	Harris, 2009, p. 119

Passengers on the Bus	Acceptance	Hayes et al., 1999, pp. 157–158
Path Up the Mountain	Values	Hayes et al., 1999, pp. 221–222
Polygraph	Control as the problem	Hayes et al., 1999, pp. 123–124
Quicksand	Control as the problem	Hayes, 2005, pp. 3–4
Shark Tank Polygraph	Control as the problem	Hayes, 2005, p. 30
Skidding	Committed action	Luoma et al., 2007, p. 170
Skiing	Values	Hayes et al., 1999, pp. 220–221
The Sky and the Weather	Self-as-context	Harris, 2009, p. 175
Swamp	Willingness	Hayes et al., 1999, pp. 247–248
Take Your Keys with You	Willingness	Hayes et al., 1999, pp. 248–250
Tug-of-War with a Monster	Control as the problem	Hayes et al., 1999, p. 109
Two Computers	Defusion	Walser & Westrup, 2007, pp. 92–94
Two Scales	Willingness	Hayes et al., 1999, pp. 133–134
We Are Fish Swimming in Our Thoughts	Defusion	Hayes, 2005, p. 55
Worm on a Hook	Acceptance	Walser & Westrup, 2007, p. 173

APPENDIX K

RIGHTS AND PERMISSIONS

Afari, Niloofar. Permission for "Mindful Walking," 2010; "Don't Think About a Puppy," 2012; and "The Traveling Partners," 2013.

Andrews, Erik, and Jill Stoddard. Permission for "The Aerospace Engineer," 2013.

Archer, Rob. Permission for "The Heroes," 2013.

Archer, Rob. Permission for "Personal Job Ad," 2013. Previously published as "Personal Job Advertisement" in *How to Find Fulfilling Work*, copyright © 2012 by Roman Krznaric and Picador, London / Macmillan. 67. Used by permission of Macmillan

A-Tjak, Jacqueline. Permission for "News of the World," 2013.

Boone, Matthew. Permission for "Value Parade," 2010. Previously published as "Label Parade" in Boone, M. S., & J. Cannici. (2013). "Acceptance and commitment therapy (ACT) in groups." In Pistorello, J. (Ed.), *Mindfulness and acceptance for counseling college students: Theory and practical applications for intervention, prevention, and outreach.* Oakland, CA: New Harbinger Publications. 73–75.

Boone, Matthew. Permission for "Willingness with an Avatar," 2010. Previously published in Boone, M. S., & J. Cannici. (2013). "Acceptance and commitment therapy (ACT) in groups." In Pistorello, J. (Ed.), *Mindfulness and acceptance for counseling college students: Theory and practical applications for intervention, prevention, and outreach.* Oakland, CA: New Harbinger Publications. 82.

Boone, Matthew. Permission for "Observing Self with Values," 2011.

Bryan, Benjamin. Permission for "Boat on the Water," 2013.

Cuneo, Jessica Gundy. Permission for "Blowing Bubbles," 2013; and "Mindfulness Diary [Appendix A]," 2013.

Dahl, Joanne C., Jennifer C. Plumb, Ian Stewart, & Tobias Lundgren, 2009. "Ten Steps to Trying on a Value." From *The art and science of valuing in psychotherapy*, copyright © 2009 by J. C. Dahl, J. C. Plumb, I. Stewart, & T. Lundgren. 164–165. Used by permission of New Harbinger Publications.

Davis, Ken. Permission for "For S/he's a Jolly Good _____," 2013; and "Life's a Beach: Struggling in the Rip," 2013.

Ferreira, Nuno, 2013. "The Bubble." Appears with permission. Previously published in Ferreira, N., & D. Gillanders. (2012). *Better living with IBS*. Wollombi, New South Wales, Australia: Exisle Publishing. 139–141.

Ferreira, Nuno, 2013. "Building a House." Appears with permission. Previously published in Ferreira, N., & D. Gillanders. (2012). *Better living with IBS*. Wollombi, New South Wales, Australia: Exisle Publishing. 27.

Ferreira, Nuno, 2013. "Zorg the Alien." Appears with permission. Previously published in Ferreira, N., & D. Gillanders. (2012). *Better living with IBS*. Wollombi, New South Wales, Australia: Exisle Publishing. 53–54.

Ferriter, Caitlin. Permission for "Crying Baby on the Plane," 2013; and "Eating an Apple," 2013.

Gammon, Taryn, & Jill Stoddard. Permission for "The Scoreboard," 2013.

Gillanders, David. Permission for "The Bicycle Factory," 2013; "The Rope Bridge," 2013; "The Sailing Boat," 2013; "Taking Off Your Armor," 2013; and "Walking the Path," 2013.

Guzman, Amber. Permission for "The Dandelion," 2013.

Harris, Russ, 2009. "Hands as Thoughts." From *ACT made simple*, copyright © 2009 by R. Harris. 20–21. Used by permission of New Harbinger Publications.

Harris, Russ, 2009. "The Master Storyteller." From *ACT made simple*, copyright © 2009 by R. Harris. 119. Used by permission of New Harbinger Publications.

Harris, Russ, 2009. "Mind-Reading Machine." From *ACT made simple*, copyright © 2009 by R. Harris. 201. Used by permission of New Harbinger Publications.

Harris, Russ, 2009. "The Sky and the Weather." From *ACT made simple*, copyright © 2009 by R. Harris. 175. Used by permission of New Harbinger Publications.

Harris, Russ, 2009. "Talking and Listening." From *ACT made simple*, copyright © 2009 by R. Harris. 177–178. Used by permission of New Harbinger Publications.

Hart, Aidan. Permission for "Waiting for the Wrong Train," 2006.

Hayes, Steven C., 2005. "Floating Leaves on a Moving Stream." From *Get out of your mind and into your life*, copyright © 2005 by S. C. Hayes & S. Smith. 76–77. Used by permission of New Harbinger Publications.

Hayes, Steven C., 2005. "Watching the Mind-Train." From *Get out of your mind and into your life*, copyright © 2005 by S. C. Hayes & S. Smith. 66–68. Used by permission of New Harbinger Publications.

Helmer, John Robert-Clyde. Permission for "Kicking Soccer Balls," 2013.

Heppner, Pia. Permission for "Holding a Pen," 2013.

Jepsen, Matthew. Permission for "Ball in a Pool," 2012.

Kates, Megan Thompson. Permission for "Observing Thoughts," 2013.

Lillis, Jason. Permission for "Responding to Triggers," 2013.

Luoma, Jason. B., Steven C. Hayes, & Robyn D. Walser, 2007. "Fusion with Self-Evaluations." From *Learning ACT*, copyright © 2007 by J. B. Luoma, S. C. Hayes, & R. D. Walser. 118–119. Used by permission of New Harbinger Publications.

Maher, Elizabeth. Permission for "ACT Thought Record [Appendix B]," 2013.

Monestès, Jean-Louis, & Matthieu Villatte, 2013. "Don't Do What You Say." Appears with permission. Previously published in French as "Ne faites pas ce que vous dites!" in Monestès, J. L., & M. Villatte. (2011). *La thérapie d'acceptation et d'engagement, ACT*. Paris, France: Elsevier Masson. 87.

O'Connell, Manuela. Permission for "Going Along with the Process," 2013.

Odhage, Mikael, 2011. "The Pendulum." Appears with permission. Previously published by the Association for Contextual Behavioral Science under Creative Commons license BY-SA. http://www.creativecommons.org/licenses/by-sa/3.0.

Randall, Fiona, & Elizabeth Burnside. Permission for "The Bag of Chips," 2013.

Rensenbrink, Nicole. Permission for "Values Words [Appendix D]," 2013.

Robb, Hank. Permission for "Understanding the Car," 2012.

Scarlet, Janina. Permission for "The Prince and the Beggar," 2013.

Schwartz, Levin. Permission for "Music, Mindfulness, and Defusion," 2013.

Sheets, Stephen, & Jill Stoddard. Permission for "The Prime-Time News Story," 2013.

Stern, Mark J. Permission for "Name That Toon," 2013; "Remodeling the House," 2013; and "Writing Your Autobiography," 2013.

Stoddard, Jill. Permission for "The Anthropologist," 2013; "Brain Bingo," 2013; "The Circus Act: Juggling and Hula Hoops," 2013; "The Classroom," 2013; "The Classroom Professor," 2013; "Conceptualized Self on Trial," 2013; "I Can't Possibly _____," 2007; "Muntu," 2007; and "Table of Values," 2007.

Titchener, 1916. "Pickle, Pickle, Pickle." Adapted from Titchener, E. B. (1916). *A beginner's guide to psychology.* New York: Macmillan. 425.

Vilatte, Matthieu, & Jean-Louis Monestès, 2013. "Say It in Another Language." Appears with permission. Previously published in French as "Dites-le dans une autre langue" in Monestès, J. L., & M. Villatte. (2011). *La thérapie d'acceptation et d'engagement, ACT.* Paris, France: Elsevier Masson. 92.

Vuille, Philippe. Permission for "The Cycling Race," 2013; and "Room Full of Duct Tape," 2013.

Walser, Robyn D., 2012. "Compassion." Appears with permission. Will appear in Walser, R. D., K. Sears, M. Chartier, & B. E. Karlin. (in press). *Acceptance and commitment therapy for depression in veterans.* Unpublished manual. Washington, DC: US Department of Veterans Affairs.

Walser, Robyn D., & Niloofar Afari. Permission for "Yes and No," 2012.

Walser, Robyn D., & Darrah Westrup, 2007. "Child." From *Acceptance and commitment therapy for the treatment of post-traumatic stress disorder,* copyright © 2007 by R. D. Walser & D. Westrup. 186–190. Used by permission of New Harbinger Publications.

Whitney, Richard. Permission for "Fly Fishing," 2013.

Wilks, Martin. Permission for "Bold Move," 2013.

Wilson, Kelly, & Troy DuFrene, 2008. "The Sweet Spot." From *Mindfulness for two,* copyright © 2009 by Kelly Wilson & Troy DuFrene. Used by permission of New Harbinger Publications.

Wilson, Randall. Permission for "Engaging the Clutch," 2013.

RESOURCES

In addition to the more general books listed in this resources section, a number of excellent diagnosis-specific manuals are available.

Foundational Texts

Hayes, S. C., Strosahl, K. D., & Wilson, K. G. (1999). *Acceptance and commitment therapy: An experiential approach to behavior change.* New York: Guilford Press.

Hayes, S. C., Strosahl, K. D., & Wilson, K. G. (2011). *Acceptance and commitment therapy, second edition: The process and practice of mindful change.* New York: Guilford Press.

Torneke, N. (2010). *Learning RFT: An introduction to relational frame theory and its clinical application.* Oakland, CA: New Harbinger.

Resources for Beginning Clinicians

Harris, R. (2009). *ACT made simple: An easy-to-read primer on acceptance and commitment therapy.* Oakland, CA: New Harbinger.

Luoma, J. B., Hayes, S. C., & Walser, R. D. (2007). *Learning ACT: An acceptance and commitment therapy skills-training manual for therapists.* Oakland, CA: New Harbinger.

Resources for All Clinicians

Bach, P. A., Moran, D. J., & Hayes, S. C. (2008). *ACT in practice: Case conceptualization in acceptance and commitment therapy.* Oakland, CA: New Harbinger.

Hayes, S. C., & Strosahl, K. D. (2004). *A practical guide to acceptance and commitment therapy.* New York: Springer.

Strosahl, K. D., Robinson, P., & Gustavsson, T. (2012). *Brief interventions for radical change: Principles and practice of focused acceptance and commitment therapy.* Oakland, CA: New Harbinger.

Wilson, K. G., & DuFrene, T. (2011). *Mindfulness for two: An acceptance and commitment therapy approach to mindfulness in psychotherapy.* Oakland, CA: New Harbinger.

Self-Help Texts for Clients

Harris, R. (2008). *The happiness trap.* Boston: Trumpeter Publications.

Hayes, S. C. (with Smith, S.). (2005). *Get out of your mind and into your life: The new acceptance and commitment therapy.* Oakland, CA: New Harbinger.

REFERENCES

Abramowitz, J. S., Tolin, D. F., & Street, G. P. (2001). Paradoxical effects of thought suppression: A meta-analysis of controlled studies. *Clinical Psychology Review, 21*, 683–703. doi:10.1016/S0272-7358(00)00057-X.

Addleman, F. G. (2004). *Get your act together: Think healthy, be healthy.* Bloomington, IN: 1st Books.

Analayo, V. (2006). Mindfulness in the Pali Nikayas. In D. K. Nauriyal, M. S. Drummond, & Y. B. Lal (Eds.), *Buddhist thought and applied psychological research: Transcending the boundaries* (pp. 229–249). London: Routledge.

Bach, P., & Hayes, S. C. (2002). The use of acceptance and commitment therapy to prevent the rehospitalization of psychotic patients: A randomized controlled trial. *Journal of Consulting and Clinical Psychology, 70*, 1129–1139. doi:10.1037//0022-006X.70.5.1129.

Baer, R. A., Fischer, S., & Huss, D. B. (2005). Mindfulness and acceptance in the treatment of disordered eating. *Journal of Rational-Emotive and Cognitive-Behavior Therapy, 23*, 281–300. doi:10.1007/s10942-005-0015-9.

Barker, P. (1985). *Using metaphors in psychotherapy.* New York: Brunner-Mazel.

Bishop, S. R., Lau, M., Shapiro, S., Carlson, L., Anderson, N. D., Carmody, J., et al. (2004). Mindfulness: A proposed operational definition. *Clinical Psychology: Science and Practice, 11*, 230–241. doi:10.1093/clipsy/bph077.

Bohlmeijer, E. T., Fledderus, M., Rokx, T. A., & Pieterse, M. E. (2011). Efficacy of an early intervention based on acceptance and commitment therapy for adults with depressive symptomatology: Evaluation in a randomized controlled trial. *Behaviour Research and Therapy, 49*, 62–67. doi:10.1016/j.brat.2010.10.003.

Boone, M. S., & Canicci, J. (2013). Acceptance and commitment therapy (ACT) in groups. In J. Pistorello (Ed.), *Mindfulness and acceptance for counseling college students: Theory and practical applications for intervention, prevention, and outreach.* Oakland, CA: New Harbinger.

Bowen, S. & Marlatt, G. A. (2009). Surfing the urge: Brief mindfulness-based intervention for college student smokers. *Psychology of Addictive Behaviors, 23,* 666–671. doi:10.1037/a0017127.

Brach, T. (2003). *Radical acceptance: Embracing your life with the heart of a Buddha.* New York: Bantam Books.

Brach, T. (2013). *True refuge: Finding peace and freedom in your own awakened heart.* New York: Bantam Books.

Brown, L. A., Forman, E. M., Herbert, J. D., Hoffman, K. L., Yuen, E. K., & Goetter, E. M. (2011). A randomized controlled trial of acceptance-based behavior therapy and cognitive therapy for test anxiety: A pilot study. *Behavior Modification, 35,* 31–53. doi:10.1177/0145445510390930.

Brown, W. B., & Ryan, R. M. (2004). Perils and promise in defining and measuring mindfulness: Observations from experience. *Clinical Psychology: Science and Practice, 11,* 242–248. doi:10.1093/clipsy/bph078.

Cahn, B. R., & Polich, J. (2006). Meditation states and traits: EEG, ERP, and neuroimaging studies. *Psychological Bulletin, 132,* 180–211. doi:10.1037/0033-2909.132.2.180.

Campbell-Sills, L., Barlow, D. H., Brown, T. A., & Hofmann, S. G. (2006). Effects of suppression and acceptance on emotional responses of individuals with anxiety and mood disorders. *Behaviour Research and Therapy, 44,* 1251–1263. doi:10.1016/j.brat.2005.10.001.

Chiesa, A., & Malinowski, P. (2011). Mindfulness-based approaches: Are they all the same? *Journal of Clinical Psychology, 67,* 404–424. doi:10.1002/jclp.20776.

Dahl, J., Plumb, J. C., Stewart, I., & Lundgren, T. (2009). *The art and science of valuing in psychotherapy: Helping clients discover, explore, and commit to valued action using acceptance and commitment therapy.* Oakland, CA: New Harbinger.

Eifert, G. H., & J. P. Forsyth. (2005). *Acceptance and commitment therapy for anxiety disorders: A practitioner's treatment guide to using mindfulness, acceptance, and values-based behavior change strategies.* Oakland, CA: New Harbinger.

Gordon, D. (1978). *Therapeutic metaphors.* Cupertino, CA: Meta Publications.

Gregg, J. A., Callaghan, G. M., Hayes, S. C., & Glenn-Lawson, J. L. (2007). Improving diabetes self-management through acceptance, mindfulness, and values: A randomized controlled trial. *Journal of Consulting and Clinical Psychology, 75,* 336–343. doi:10.1037/0022-006X.75.2.336.

Harris, R. (2009). *ACT made simple: An easy-to-read primer on acceptance and commitment therapy.* Oakland, CA: New Harbinger.

Hayes, S. C. (with Smith, S.). (2005). *Get out of your mind and into your life: The new acceptance and commitment therapy.* Oakland, CA: New Harbinger.

Hayes, S. C., Barnes-Holmes, D., & Roche, B. (2001). *Relational frame theory: A post-Skinnerian account of human language and cognition.* New York: Plenum.

Hayes, S. C., Strosahl, K. D., & Wilson, K. G. (1999). *Acceptance and commitment therapy: An experiential approach to behavior change.* New York: Guilford Press.

Hayes, S. C., Strosahl, K. D., & Wilson, K. G. (2011). *Acceptance and commitment therapy, second edition: The process and practice of mindful change.* New York: Guilford Press.

Hayes, S. C., Villatte, M., Levin, M., & Hildebrandt, M. (2011). Open, aware, and active: Contextual approaches as an emerging trend in the behavioral and cognitive therapies. *Annual Review of Clinical Psychology, 7,* 141–168. doi:10.1146/annurevclinpsy-032210-104449.

Hayes, S. C., Wilson, K. G., Gifford, E. V., Bissett, R., Piasecki, M., Batten, S. V., et al. (2004). A randomized controlled trial of twelve-step facilitation and acceptance and commitment therapy with polysubstance-abusing methadone-maintained opiate addicts. *Behavior Therapy, 35,* 667–688. doi:10.1016/S0005-7894(04)80014-5.

Jinpa, G. T. (2010). Compassion cultivation training (CCT): Instructor's manual (unpublished).

Juarascio, A. S., Forman, E. M., & Herbert, J. D. (2010). Acceptance and commitment therapy versus cognitive therapy for the treatment of comorbid eating pathology. *Behavior Modification, 34,* 175–190. doi:10.1177/0145445510363472.

Kabat-Zinn, J. (1991). *Full catastrophe living: Using the wisdom of your body and mind to face stress, pain, and illness.* New York: Delta.

Kabat-Zinn, J. (1994). *Wherever you go there you are: Mindfulness meditation in everyday life.* New York: Hyperion.

Kabat-Zinn, J. (2011). *Mindfulness for beginners: Reclaiming the present moment—and your life.* Boulder, CO: Sounds True.

Kingsolver, B. (1998). *The poisonwood bible.* New York: Harper Perennial Modern Classics.

Kiyota, M. (1978). *Mahayana Buddhist meditation: Theory and practice.* Honolulu: University Press of Hawaii.

Kohlenberg, R. J., & Tsai, M. (1991). *Functional analytic psychotherapy: A guide for creating intense and curative therapeutic relationships.* New York: Plenum.

Krznaric, R. (2012). *How to find fulfilling work: The school of life.* London: Macmillan.

Linehan, M. M. (1993a). *Cognitive-behavioral treatment of borderline personality disorder.* New York: Guilford Press.

Linehan, M. M. (1993b). *Skills training manual for treating borderline personality disorder.* New York: Guilford Press.

Lipkens, R., & Hayes, S. C. (2009). Producing and recognizing analogical relations. *Journal of the Experimental Analysis of Behavior, 91,* 105–126. doi:10.1901/jeab.2009.91-105.

Luoma, J. B., Hayes, S. C., & Walser, R. D. (2007). *Learning ACT: An acceptance and commitment therapy skills-training manual for therapists.* Oakland, CA: New Harbinger.

McKay, M., Wood, J., & Brantley, J. (2007). *The dialectical behavior therapy skills workbook: Practical DBT exercises for learning mindfulness, interpersonal effectiveness, emotion regulation, and distress tolerance.* Oakland, CA: New Harbinger.

Monestès, J. L., & Villatte, M. (2011). *La thérapie d'acceptation et d'engagement ACT.* Paris, France: Elsevier-Masson.

O'Hora, D., Barnes-Holmes, D., Roche, B., & Smeets, P. M. (2004). Derived relational networks and control by novel instructions: A possible model of generative verbal responding. *Psychological Record, 54,* 437–460. Retrieved from http://opensiuc.lib.siu.edu/tpr.

Perls, F., Hefferline, R., & Goodman, P. (1951). *Gestalt therapy: Excitement and growth in the human personality.* New York: Julian.

Polster, E. & Polster, M. (1973). *Gestalt therapy integrated: Contours of theory and practice.* New York: Brunner-Mazel.

Rapygay, L., & Bystrisky, A. (2009). Classical mindfulness: An introduction to its theory and practice for clinical application. *Annals of the New York Academy of Science, 1172,* 148–162. doi:10.1111/j.1749-6632.2009.04405.x.

Robinson, P. J. & Strosahl, K. D. (2008). *The mindfulness and acceptance workbook for depression: Using acceptance and commitment therapy to move through depression and create a life worth living.* Oakland, CA: New Harbinger.

Roemer, L., Orsillo, S. M., & Salters-Pedneault, K. (2008). Efficacy of an acceptance-based behavior therapy for generalized anxiety disorder: Evaluation in a randomized controlled trial. *Journal of Consulting and Clinical Psychology, 76,* 1083–1089. doi:10.1037/a0012720.

Rosen, S. (Ed.). (1982). *My voice will go with you: The teaching tales of Milton H. Erickson, M.D.* New York: Norton.

Segal, Z. V., Williams, J. M. G., & Teasdale, J. D. (2002). *Mindfulness-based cognitive therapy for depression: A new approach to preventing relapse.* New York: Guilford Press.

Smout, M., Longo, M., Harrison, S., Minniti, R., Wickes, W., & White, J. (2010). Psychosocial treatment for methamphetamine use disorders: A preliminary randomized controlled trial of cognitive behavior therapy and acceptance and commitment therapy. *Substance Abuse, 31,* 98–107. doi:10.1080/08897071003641578.

Stewart, I., Barnes-Holmes, D., Hayes, S. C., & Lipkens, R. (2001). Relations among relations: Analogies, metaphors, and stories. In S. C. Hayes, D. Barnes-Holmes, & B. Roche (Eds.), *Relational frame theory: A post-Skinnerian account of language and cognition* (pp. 73–86). New York: Plenum.

Titchener, E. B. (1916). *A beginner's psychology.* New York: Macmillan.

Twohig, M. P., Hayes, S. C., & Masuda, A. (2006). A preliminary investigation of acceptance and commitment therapy as a treatment for chronic skin picking. *Behaviour Research and Therapy, 44,* 1513–1522. doi:10.1016/j.brat.2005.10.002.

Vøllestad, J., Nielsen, M. B., & Nielsen, G. H. (2011). Mindfulness- and acceptance-based interventions for anxiety disorders: A systematic review and meta-analysis. *British Journal of Clinical Psychology, 51,* 239–260.doi:10.1111/j.2044-8260.2011.02024.x.

Vowles, K. E., & McCracken, L. M. (2008). Acceptance and values-based action in chronic pain: A study of treatment effectiveness and process. *Journal of Consulting and Clinical Psychology, 76,* 397–407. doi:10.1037/0022-006X.76.3.397.

Walser, R. D., Sears, K., Chartier, M., & Karlin, B. E. (in press). *Acceptance and commitment therapy for depression in veterans: Therapist manual.* Washington, DC: US Department of Veterans Affairs.

Walser, R. D., & Westrup, D. (2007). *Acceptance and commitment therapy for the treatment of post-traumatic stress disorder: A practitioner's guide to using mindfulness and acceptance strategies.* Oakland, CA: New Harbinger.

Westin, V. Z., Schulin, M., Hesser, H., Karlsson, M., Noe, R. Z., Olofsson, U., et al. (2011). Acceptance and commitment therapy versus tinnitus retraining therapy in the treatment of tinnitus distress: A randomized controlled trial. *Behaviour Research and Therapy, 49,* 737–747. doi:10.1016/j.brat.2011.08.001.

Wetherell, J. L., Afari, N., Rutledge, T., Sorrell, J. T., Stoddard, J. A., Petkus, A. J., et al. (2011a). A randomized, controlled trial of acceptance and commitment therapy and cognitive-behavioral therapy for chronic pain. *Pain, 152,* 2098–2107. doi:10.1016/j.pain.2011.05.016.

Wetherell, J. L., Afari, N., Ayers, C. R., Stoddard, J. A., Ruberg, J., Sorrell, J. T., et al. (2011b). Acceptance and commitment therapy for generalized anxiety disorder in older adults: A preliminary report. *Behavior Therapy, 42,* 127–134. doi:10.1016/j.beth.2010.07.002.

Wilson, K. G., Bordieri, M. J., Flynn, M. K., Lucas, N. N., & Slater, R. M. (2011). Understanding acceptance and commitment therapy in context: A history of similarities and differences with other cognitive behavior therapies. In J. D. Herbert & E. M. Forman (Eds.), *Acceptance and mindfulness in cognitive behavior therapy: Understanding and applying the new therapies* (pp. 233–264). Hoboken, NJ: John Wiley and Sons.

Wilson, K. G., & DuFrene, T. (2009). *Mindfulness for two: An acceptance and commitment therapy approach to mindfulness in psychotherapy.* Oakland, CA: New Harbinger.

Zettle, R. D. (2007). *ACT for depression: A clinician's guide to using acceptance and commitment therapy in treating depression.* Oakland, CA: New Harbinger.

Zettle, R. D., & Rains, J. C. (1989). Group cognitive and contextual therapies in treatment of depression. *Journal of Clinical Psychology, 45,* 436–445. doi:10.1002/1097-4679(198905)45:3--436::AID-JCLP2270450314--3.0.CO;2-L.

Jill A. Stoddard, PhD, is the founder and director of The Center for Stress and Anxiety Management, an outpatient clinic in San Diego, CA. She specializes in evidence-based treatments for anxiety and related disorders, and is associate professor of psychology at Alliant International University where she teaches, conducts research, and mentors students in topics related to anxiety disorders; trauma; emotion regulation; acceptance and commitment therapy (ACT); and cognitive behavioral therapy (CBT). She received her PhD in clinical psychology from Boston University in 2007.

Niloofar Afari, PhD, is an associate professor of psychiatry at the University of California, San Diego; director of Mental Health Integrative and Consultative Services at VA San Diego Healthcare System; and director of Clinical Research at the VA Center of Excellence for Stress and Mental Health in San Diego, CA. In addition to clinical practice, she conducts research and mentors graduate and postdoctoral students in the application of ACT to chronic health conditions. She received her PhD in clinical psychology in 1996 from the University of Nevada, Reno, under the mentorship of ACT cofounder, Steven C. Hayes.

Foreword writer **Steven C. Hayes, PhD**, is Nevada Foundation Professor in the department of psychology at the University of Nevada. An author of thirty-four books and more than 470 scientific articles, he has shown in his research how language and thought leads to human suffering, and cofounded ACT, a powerful therapy method that is useful in a wide variety of areas. Hayes has been president of several scientific societies and has received several national awards, including the Lifetime Achievement Award from the Association for Behavioral and Cognitive Therapy.

INDEX

A

about this book, 2–4

acceptance, 29, 33–35, 45–61; ACT process of, 8; behavioral flexibility and, 33–34; building metaphors for, 20; compassion and, 50; description of, 29; direct experience of, 15; experiential avoidance vs., 29; metaphors/ exercises targeting, 45–57, 59–61; strategies to support, 35–57; for therapists, 35. *See also* willingness

acceptance and commitment therapy (ACT): definition of, 1; disorders treated with, 1–2; experiential techniques used in, 14–16; guidelines for using metaphors and exercises in, 170–173; hexaflex diagrams used in, 7, 12; list of additional exercises/metaphors, 201–206; mindfulness in, 14–15, 86–87; multiple processes addressed in, 173–176; psychological flexibility and, 11–12; recommended resources for, 176–177, 211– 212; role of metaphors and exercises in, 2, 169–170; six core therapeutic processes in, 7–11

Acceptance and Commitment Therapy: An Experiential Approach to Behavior Change (Hayes et al.), 176

Acceptance and Commitment Therapy for Depression in Veterans (Walser et al.), 50

acceptance and willingness metaphors/ exercises, 45–57, 59–61; Child exercise, 52–54; Compassion exercise, 50–51; Crying Baby on a Plane metaphor, 55; Eating an Apple metaphor, 54; Engaging the Clutch metaphor, 56–57; Holding a Pen exercise, 47–49; Understanding the Car metaphor, 56; Willingness with an Avatar exercise, 102–103; Yes and No exercise, 46–47

ACT Made Simple (Harris), 102

ACT Thought Record, 89, 181–182

action plans: developing goals and, 152–153. *See also* committed action

Aerospace Engineer metaphor, 146

Afari, Niloofar, 36, 46, 90, 161

agenda, therapeutic, 171

Andrews, Erik, 146

Anthropologist metaphor, 124

anxiety: Going Along with the Process exercise for, 94–96; Life's a Beach script for, 43–44

Archer, Rob, 132, 141, 187
Association for Contextual Behavioral
   Science (ACBS), 3
A-Tjak, Jacqueline, 77
autobiography writing exercise, 136–137,
   189–190
avoidance. *See* experiential avoidance
awareness. *See* present-moment awareness

B

Bag of Chips exercise, 93–94
Ball in a Pool metaphor, 39
barriers to action, 153–154
behaviors: flexibility of, 33–34; metaphors for
   problematic, 18–19
Bicycle Factory metaphor, 165–166
Blind Writing exercise, 19
Blowing Bubbles exercise, 98–99
Boat on the Water exercise, 70–71
body-scan exercise, 14
Bold Move exercise, 159–160
Boone, Matthew, 99, 102, 114
Brach, Tara, 46, 176
Brain Bingo exercise, 78–79
Bryan, Benjamin, 70
Bubble exercise, 158–159; graphics and
   worksheet for, 197–199
Building a House metaphor, 40–41
building therapeutic metaphors, 19–21
Burnside, Elizabeth, 93

C

change agenda, 35
Chessboard metaphor, 119
Child exercise, 52–54
Circus Act metaphor, 44–45
Classroom metaphor, 120

Classroom Professor metaphor, 144–145;
   graphics and worksheet for, 193–195
clean pain, 30, 34
clients: delivering metaphors to, 21–27;
   introducing mindfulness to, 87–89;
   seeking permission from, 173; self-help
   texts for, 212
cognitive defusion. *See* defusion
cognitive fusion. *See* fusion
committed action, 151–168; ACT core
   process of, 10–11; barriers to, 153–154;
   building larger patterns of, 155–157;
   exercises supporting, 157–160, 167–168;
   explanation and example of, 151–152;
   forms vs. functions of, 154–155; goals and
   action plans for, 152–153; metaphors
   targeting, 160–166, 167, 168; worksheet on
   values and, 191–192
committed action exercises, 157–160, 167–
   168; Bold Move, 159–160; The Bubble,
   158–159, 197–199; Zorg the Alien,
   157–158
committed action metaphors, 160–166, 167,
   168; The Bicycle Factory, 165–166; The
   Rope Bridge, 163; The Traveling Partners,
   161; Waiting for the Wrong Train, 162;
   Walking the Path, 164
Compassion exercise, 50–51
concentrative meditation, 85
conceptualized self, 109–111, 118–119
Conceptualized Self on Trial exercise,
   118–119
control: metaphors/exercises for dealing with,
   35–45, 59–61; problem with efforts
   involving, 29–30; therapeutic agenda of,
   35; verbal forms of, 14–15
control as the problem metaphors/exercises,
   35–45, 59–61; Ball in a Pool metaphor, 39;
   Building a House metaphor, 40–41; Circus

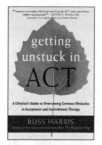
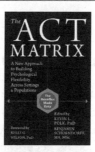

MANY VOICES | ONE WORK

A subsidiary of New Harbinger Publications, Inc.

Enhance your practice with live ACT workshops

Praxis Continuing Education and Training—a subsidiary of New Harbinger Publications—is the premier provider of evidence-based continuing education for mental health professionals. Praxis specializes in ongoing **acceptance and commitment therapy (ACT)** training—taught by leading ACT experts. Praxis workshops are designed to help professionals learn and effectively implement ACT in session with clients.

ACT BootCamp®: Introduction to Implementation

For professionals with no prior experience with ACT, as well as those who want to refresh their knowledge

Learn the foundations of the psychological flexibility model, and develop a beginning set of skills in acceptance and commitment therapy (ACT). Understand the basics of relational frame theory (RFT)—the theory of language and cognition on which ACT is built. See, do, get feedback. Get hands-on, guided practice recognizing psychological inflexibility in clients in real time, and learn to fluidly respond from all points on the hexaflex. Dig into how ACT reinvigorates your therapeutic relationship with clients. Close with one day of practical review of what you've learned, reinforcing tools and techniques for working with clients. For total ACT immersion, attend evening sessions to learn from ACT experts to get your questions answered and build community.

ACT 1: Introduction to ACT

For professionals with no prior experience with ACT

Learn the foundations of the psychological flexibility model, and develop a beginning set of skills in acceptance and commitment therapy (ACT). See, do, get feedback. Dive into relational frame theory (RFT)—the theory of language and cognition on which ACT is built. Learn the hexaflex (flexible contact with the present moment, cognitive defusion, acceptance, self-as-context, values, committed action) and the basic processes of ACT while adding ACT metaphors and techniques to your therapeutic toolbox.

CONCEPTUAL | EXPERIENTIAL | PRACTICAL

ACT 2: Clinical Skills-Building Intensive

For professionals who practice ACT, but want more hands-on experience

This skills-building intensive includes round after round of interactive, experiential exercises. You will see, do, and get feedback as you build a solid basis in the dynamic use of acceptance and commitment therapy (ACT) interventions. The outcome? A better understanding of the model, and the ability to recognize inflexibility in clients and respond in real time. The net result: better clinical outcomes.

ACT 3: Mastering ACT

For professionals actively using ACT who want to apply it to their most complex cases

This master class is about the art and science of doing acceptance and commitment therapy (ACT) well with all of your clients. Bring your most difficult cases into the training, and work with master ACT trainers to resolve your biggest challenges. Develop an understanding of the intra- and interpersonal processes that happen inside the therapy room. Develop a deeper understanding of how your own behaviors impact yourself, as well as your clients in the therapy room. Get intensive practice conducting functional analysis in the moment, and then apply ACT solutions to your findings.

Receive 10% off Any Training!

Visit praxiscet.com and use code **EDU10** at checkout to receive 10% off.

Can't make a workshop? Check out our online and on-demand courses at **praxiscet.com**

Register your **new harbinger** titles for additional benefits!

When you register your **new harbinger** title—purchased in any format, from any source—you get access to benefits like the following:

- Downloadable accessories like printable worksheets and extra content
- Instructional videos and audio files
- Information about updates, corrections, and new editions

Not every title has accessories, but we're adding new material all the time.

Access free accessories in 3 easy steps:

1. Sign in at NewHarbinger.com (or **register** to create an account).

2. Click on **register a book**. Search for your title and click the **register** button when it appears.

3. Click on the **book cover or title** to go to its details page. Click on **accessories** to view and access files.

That's all there is to it!

If you need help, visit:

NewHarbinger.com/accessories

new harbinger
CELEBRATING
40 YEARS